Georg Ebers, Mary Joanna Safford

Cleopatra

A Romance

Georg Ebers, Mary Joanna Safford

Cleopatra
A Romance

ISBN/EAN: 9783744777230

Printed in Europe, USA, Canada, Australia, Japan

Cover: Foto ©ninafisch / pixelio.de

More available books at **www.hansebooks.com**

A ROMANCE

BY
GEORG EBERS
AUTHOR OF UARDA, AN EGYPTIAN PRINCESS, SERAPIS, JOSHUA,
A THORNY PATH, THE STORY OF MY LIFE, ETC.

TRANSLATED FROM THE GERMAN
By MARY J. SAFFORD

IN TWO VOLUMES
VOL. II

NEW YORK
D. APPLETON AND COMPANY
1894

COPYRIGHT, 1894,
BY D. APPLETON AND COMPANY.

ELECTROTYPED AND PRINTED
AT THE APPLETON PRESS, U.S.A.

CLEOPATRA.

CHAPTER XIII.

During these hours of rest Iras and Charmian had watched in turn beside Cleopatra. When she rose, the younger attendant rendered her the necessary services. She was to devote herself to her mistress until the evening; for her companion, who now stood in her way, was not to return earlier. Before Charmian left, she had seen that her apartments—in which Barine, since the Queen had placed her in her charge, had been a welcome guest—were carefully watched. The commander of the Macedonian guard, who years before had vainly sought her favour, and finally had become the most loyal of her friends, had promised to keep them closely.

Yet Iras knew how to profit by her mistress's sleep and the absence of her aunt. She had learned that she would be shut out of her apartments, and therefore from Barine also. Ere any step could be taken against the prisoner, she must first arrange the necessary preliminaries with Alexas. The failure of her expectation of seeing her rival trampled in the dust had transformed her jealous resentment into hatred, and though she was her niece, she even transferred a portion of it to Charmian, who had placed herself between her and her victim.

She had sent for the Syrian, but he, too, had gone to rest at a late hour and kept her waiting a long time. The reception which the impatient girl bestowed was therefore by no means cordial, but her manner soon grew more friendly.

First Alexas boasted of having induced the Queen to commit Barine's fate to him. If he should try her at noon and find her guilty, there was nothing to prevent him from compelling her to drink the poisoned cup or having her strangled before evening. But the matter would be dangerous, because the singer's friends were numerous and by no means powerless. Yet, in the depths of her heart, Cleopatra desired nothing more ardently than to rid herself of her dangerous rival. But he knew the great ones of the earth. If he acted energetically and brought matters to a speedy close, the Queen, to avoid evil gossip, would burden him with her own act. Antony's mood could not be predicted, and the Syrian's weal or woe depended on his favour. Besides, the execution of the singer at the last Adonis festival might have a dangerous effect upon the people of Alexandria. They were already greatly excited, and his brother, who knew them, said that some were overwhelmed with sorrow, and others ready, in their fury, to rise in a bloody rebellion. Everything was to be feared from this rabble, but Philostratus understood how to persuade them to many things, and Alexas had just secured his aid.

Alexas had really succeeded in the work of reconciliation. During the orator's married life with Barine she had forbidden her brother-in-law the house, and her husband had quarrelled with the brother who sought his wife. But after the latter had risen to a high place in Antony's favour, and been loaded with gold by his lavish hand, Philostratus had again approached him to claim his share of the new wealth. And the source from which Alexas drew flowed so abundantly that his favourite did not find it difficult to give. Both men were as unprincipled as they were lavish, and experience taught them that base natures always have at their disposal a plank with which to bridge chasms. If it is of gold, it will be crossed the more speedily. Such was the case here, and of late it had become specially firm; for each needed the other's aid.

Alexas loved Barine, while Philostratus no longer cared for her. On the other hand, he hated Dion with so ardent a thirst for revenge that, to obtain it, he would have resigned even the hope of fresh gains. The humiliation inflicted upon him by the arrogant Macedonian noble, and the derision which through his efforts had been heaped upon him, haunted him like importunate pursuers; and he felt that he could only rid himself of them with the source of his disgrace. Without his brother's aid, he would have been content to assail Dion with his slandering tongue; with his powerful assistance he could inflict a heavier injury upon him, perhaps even rob him of liberty and life. They had just made an agreement by which Philostratus pledged himself to reconcile the populace to any punishment that might be inflicted upon Barine, and Alexas promised to help his brother take a bloody vengeance upon Dion the Macedonian.

Barine's death could be of no service to Alexas. The sight of her beauty had fired his heart a second time, and he was resolved to make her his own. In the dungeon, perhaps by torture, she should be forced to grasp his helping hand. All this would permit no delay. Everything must be done before the return of Antony, who was daily expected. Alexas's lavish patron had made him so rich that he could bear to lose his favour for the sake of this object. Even without it, he could maintain a household with royal magnificence in some city of his Syrian home.

On receiving the favourite's assurance that he would remove Barine from Charmian's protection on the morrow, Iras became more gracious. She could make no serious objection to his statement that the new trial might not, it is true, end in a sentence of death, but the verdict would probably be transportation to the mines, or something of the sort.

Then Alexas cautiously tested Iras's feelings towards his brother's mortal foe. They were hostile; yet when the favourite intimated that he, too, ought to be given up to justice, she showed so much hesitation, that Alexas stopped abruptly and turned the conversation upon Barine. Here she promised assistance with her former eager zeal, and it was settled that the arrest should be made the following morning during the hours of Charmian's attendance upon the Queen.

Iras had valuable counsel to offer. She was familiar with one of the prisons, whose doors she had opened to many a hapless mortal whose disappearance, in her opinion, might be of service to the Queen. She had deemed it a duty, aided by the Keeper of the Seal, to anticipate her mistress in cases where her kind heart would have found it difficult to pronounce a severe sentence, and Cleopatra had permitted it, though without commendation or praise. What happened within its walls—thanks to the silence of the warder—never passed beyond the portals. If Barine cursed her life there, she would still fare better than she, Iras, who during the past few nights had been on the brink of despair whenever she thought of the man who had disdained her love and abandoned her for another.

As the Syrian held out his hand to take leave, she asked bluntly:

"And Dion?"

"He cannot be set free," was the reply, "for he loves Barine; nay, the fool was on the eve of leading her home to his beautiful palace as its mistress."

"Is that true, really true?" asked Iras, whose cheeks and lips lost every tinge of colour, though she succeeded in maintaining her composure.

"He confessed it yesterday in a letter to his uncle, the Keeper of the Seal, in which he entreated him to do his utmost for his chosen bride, whom he would never resign. But Zeno has no liking for this niece. Do you wish to see the letter?"

"Then, of course, he cannot be set at liberty," replied Iras, and there was additional shrillness in her voice. "He will do everything in his power for the woman he loves, and that is much—far more than you, who are half a stranger here, suspect. The Macedonian families stand by each other. He is a member of the council. The bands of the Ephebi will support him to a man. And the populace?—He lately spoiled the game of your brother, who was acting for me, in a way.— He was finally dragged out of the basin of the fountain, dripping with water and overwhelmed with shame."

"For that very reason his mouth must be closed."

Iras nodded assent, but after a short pause she exclaimed angrily: "I will help you to silence him, but not forever. Do you hear? Theodotus's saying about the dead dogs which do not bite brought no blessing to any one who followed it. There are other ways of getting rid of this man."

"A bird sang that you were not unfriendly to him."

"A bird? Then it was probably an owl, which cannot see in the daylight. His worst enemy, your brother, would probably sacrifice himself for his welfare sooner than I."

"Then I shall begin to feel sympathy for this Dion."

"I saw recently that your compassion surpassed mine. Death is not the hardest punishment."

"Is that the cause of this gracious respite?"

"Perhaps so. But there are other matters to be considered here. First, the condition of the times. Everything is tottering, even the royal power, which a short time ago was a wall which concealed many things and afforded shelter from every assault. Then Dion himself. I have already numbered those who will support him. Since the defeat at Actium, the Queen can no longer exclaim to that many-headed monster, the people, 'You must,' but 'I entreat.' The others——"

"The first considerations are enough; but may I be permitted to know what my wise friend has awarded to the hapless wight from whom she withdrew her favour?"

"First, imprisonment here at Lochias. He has stained his hands with the blood of Cæsarion, the King of kings. That is high treason, even in the eyes of the people. Try to obtain the order for the arrest this very day."

"Whenever I can disturb the Queen with such matters."

"Not for *my* sake, but to save *her* from injury. Away with everything which can cloud her intellect in these decisive days! First, away with Barine, who spoiled her return home; and then let us take care of the man who would be capable, for this woman's sake, of causing an insurrection in Alexandria. The great cares associated with the state and the throne are hers; for the minor ones of the toilet and the heart I will provide."

Here she was interrupted by one of Cleopatra's waiting-maids. The Queen had awakened, and Iras hastened to her post.

As she passed Charmian's apartments and saw two handsome soldiers, belonging to the Macedonian body-guard, pacing to and fro on duty before them, her face darkened. It was against her alone that Charmian was protecting Barine. She had been harshly reproved by the older woman on account of the artist's daughter, who had been the source of so many incidents which had caused her pain, and Iras regretted that she had ever confided to her aunt her love for Dion. But, no matter what might happen, the upas-tree whence emanated all these tortures, anxieties, and vexations, must be rooted out—stricken from the ranks of the living.

Ere she entered the Queen's anteroom she had mentally pronounced sentence of death on her enemy. Her inventive brain was now busy in devising means to induce the Syrian to undertake its execution. If this stone of offence was removed it would again be possible to live in harmony with Charmian. Dion would be free, and then, much as he had wounded her, she would defend him from the hatred of Philostratus and his brother.

She entered the Queen's presence with a lighter heart. The death of a condemned person had long since ceased to move her deeply. While rendering the first services to her mistress, who had been much refreshed by her sleep, her face grew brighter and brighter; for Cleopatra voluntarily told her that she was glad to have her attendance, and not be constantly annoyed by the same disagreeable matter, which must soon be settled.

In fact, Charmian, conscious that no one else at court would have ventured to do so, had never grown weary, spite of many a rebuff, of pleading Barine's cause until, the day before, Cleopatra, in a sudden fit of anger, had commanded her not to mention the mischief-maker again.

When Charmian soon after requested permission to let Iras take her place the following day, the Queen already regretted the harsh reproof she had given her friend, and, while cordially granting the desired leave, begged her to attribute her angry impatience to the cares which burdened her. "And when you show me your kind, faithful face again," she concluded, "you will have remembered that a true friend withholds from an unhappy woman whom she loves whatever will shadow more deeply her already clouded life. This Barine's very name sounds like a jeer at the composure I maintain with so much difficulty. I do not wish to hear it again."

The words were uttered in a tone so affectionate and winning, that Charmian's vexation melted like ice in the sun. Yet she left the Queen's presence anxious and troubled; for ere she quitted the room Cleopatra remarked that she had committed the singer's affairs to Alexas. She was now doubly eager to obtain a day's freedom, for she knew the unprincipled favourite's feelings towards the young beauty, and longed to discuss with Archibius the best means of guarding her from the worst perils.

When at a late hour she went to rest, she was served by the Nubian maid, who had accompanied her to the court from her parents' home. She came from the Cataract, where she had been bought when the family of Alypius accompanied the child Cleopatra to the island of Philæ. Anukis was given to Charmian, who at the time was just entering womanhood, as the first servant who was her sole property, and she had proved so clever, skilful, apt to learn, and faithful, that her mistress took her, as her personal attendant, to the palace.

Charmian's warm, unselfish love for the Queen was equalled by Anukis's devotion to the mistress who had long since made her free, and had become so strongly attached to her that the Nubian's interests were little less regarded than her own. Her sound, keen judgment and natural wit had gained a certain renown in the palace, and as Cleopatra often condescended to rouse her to an apt answer, Antony had done so, too; and since the slight crook in the back, which she had from childhood, had grown into a hump, he gave her the name of Aisopion—the female Æsop. All the Queen's attendants now used it, and though others of lower rank did the same, she permitted it, though her ready wit would have supplied her tongue with a retort sharp enough to respond to any word which displeased her.

But she knew the life and fables of Æsop, who had also once been a slave, and deemed it an honour to be compared with him.

When Charmian had left Cleopatra and sought her chamber, she found Barine sound asleep, but Anukis was awaiting her, and her mistress told her with what deep anxiety for Barine she had quitted the presence of the Queen. She knew that the Nubian was fond of the young matron, whom in her childhood she had carried in her arms, and whose father, Leonax, had often jested with her. The maid had watched her career with much interest, and while Barine had been her mistress's guest her efforts to amuse and soothe her were unceasing.

She had gone every morning to Berenike to ask tidings of Dion's health, and always brought favourable news. Anukis knew Philostratus and his brother, too, and as she liked Antony, who jested with her so kindly, she grieved to see an unprincipled fellow like Alexas his chief confidant. She knew the plots with which the Syrian had persecuted Barine, and when Charmian told her that the Queen had committed the young beauty's fate to this man's keeping her dark face grew fairly livid; but she forced herself to conceal the terror which the news inspired. Her mistress was also aware what this choice meant to Barine. But Anukis would have thought it wrong to disturb Charmian's sleep by revealing her own distress. It was fortunate that she was going early the next morning to seek the aid of Archibius, whom Anukis believed to be the wisest of men; but this by no means soothed her. She knew the fable of the lion and the mouse, which had been told in her home long before the time of the author for whom she was nicknamed, and already more than once she had been in a position to render far greater and more powerful persons an important service. To soothe Charmian to sleep and turn her thoughts in another direction, she told her about Dion, whom she had found much better that day, how tenderly he seemed to love Barine, and how touchingly patient and worthy of her father the daughter of Leonax had been.

After her mistress had fallen asleep she went to the hall where, spite of the late hour, she expected to meet some of the servants—sure of being greeted as a welcome guest. When, a short time later, Alexas's body-slave appeared, she filled his wine cup, sat down by his side, and tried with all the powers at her command to win his confidence. And so well did the elderly Nubian succeed that Marsyas, a handsome young Ligurian, after she had gone, declared that Aisopion's jokes and stories were enough to bring the dead to life, and it was as pleasant to talk seriously with the brown-skinned monster as to dally with a fair-haired sweetheart.

After Charmian had left the palace the following morning, Anukis again sought Marsyas and learned from him for what purpose and at what hour Iras had summoned Alexas. His master was continually whispering with the languishing Macedonian.

When Anukis returned, Barine seemed troubled because she brought no tidings from her mother and Dion; but the Nubian entreated her to have patience, and gave her some books and a spindle, that she might have occupation in her solitude. She, Anukis, must go to the kitchen, because she had heard yesterday that the cook had bought some mushrooms, which might be poisonous; she knew the fungi and wanted to see them.

Then, passing into Charmian's chamber, she glided through the corridor which connected the apartments of Cleopatra's confidential attendants, and slipped into Iras's room. When Alexas entered she was concealed behind one of the hangings which covered the walls of the reception-room.

After the Syrian had retired and Iras had been called away, Anukis returned to Barine and said that the mushrooms had really been poisonous, and of the deadliest species. They had been cooked, and she must go out to seek an antidote. Since a precious human life might be at stake, Barine would not wish to keep her.

"Go," said the latter, kindly. "But if you are the old obliging Aisopion, you won't object to going a little farther."

"And inquiring at the house near the Paneum garden," added Anukis. "That was already settled. Longing is also a poison for a loving heart, and its antidote is good news."

With these laughing words she left her favourite; but as soon as she was out of doors her black brow became lined with earnest thought, and she stood pondering a long time. At last she went to the Bruchium to hire a donkey to ride to Kanopus, where she hoped to find Archibius. It was difficult to reach the nearest stand; for a great crowd had assembled on the quay between the Lochias and the Corner of the Muses, and groups of the common people, sailors, and slaves were constantly flocking hither. But she at last forced her way to the spot and, while the driver was helping her to mount the animal she had chosen, she asked what had attracted the throng, and he answered:

"They are tearing down the house of the old Museum fungus, Didymus."

"How can that be?" cried the startled woman. "The good old man!"

"Good?" repeated the driver, scornfully. "He's a traitor, who has caused all the trouble. Philostratus, the brother of the great Alexas, a friend of Mark Antony, told us so. He wanted to prove it, so it must be true. Hear the shouts, and how the stones are flying! Yes, yes. His granddaughter and her lover set an ambush for the King Cæsarion. They would have killed him, but the watch interfered, and now he lies wounded on his couch. If mighty Isis does not lend her aid, the young prince's life will soon be over."

Then, turning to the donkey, he dealt him two severe blows on the right and left haunches, shouting: "Hi, Grey! It does one good to hear that royal backs have room for the cudgel too."

Meanwhile, the Nubian was hesitating whether she should not first turn the donkey to the right and seek Didymus; but Barine was threatened by greater peril, and her life was of more value than the welfare of the aged pair. This decided the question, and she rode forward.

The donkey and his driver did their best, but they came too late; for in the little palace at Kanopus, Anukis learned from the porter that Archibius had gone to the city with his old friend Timagenes, the historian, who lived in Rome, and seemed to have come to Alexandria as an envoy.

Charmian, too, had been here, but also failed to find the master of the house, and followed him. Evil tidings—which, owing to the loss of time involved, might prove fatal. If the donkey had only been swifter! True, Archibius's stable was full of fine animals, but who was she that she should presume to use them? Yet she had gained something which rendered her the equal of many who were born free and occupied a higher station—the reputation for trustworthiness and wisdom; and relying upon this, she told the faithful old steward, as far as possible, what was at stake, and soon after he himself took her, both mounted on swift mules, to the city and the Paneum garden.

He chose the nearest road thither through the Gate of the Sun and the Kanopic Way. Usually at this hour it was crowded with people, but to-day few persons were astir. All the idlers had thronged to the Bruchium and the harbour to see the returning ships of the vanquished fleet, hear something new, witness the demonstrations of joy, the sacrifices and processions, and—if Fortune favoured—meet the Queen and relieve their overflowing hearts by acclamations.

When the carriage turned towards the left and approached the Paneum, progress for the first time became difficult. A dense crowd had gathered around the hill on whose summit the sanctuary of Pan dominated the spacious garden. Anukis's eye perceived the tall figure of Philostratus. Was the mischief-maker everywhere? This time he seemed to encounter opposition, for loud shouts interrupted his words. Just as the carriage passed he pointed to the row of houses in which the widow of Leonax lived, but violent resistance followed the gesture.

Anukis perceived what restrained the crowd; for, as the equipage approached its destination, a body of armed youths stopped it. Their finely-formed limbs, steeled by the training of the Palæstra, and the raven, chestnut, and golden locks floating around their well-shaped heads, were indeed beautiful. They were a band of the Ephebi, formerly commanded by Archibius, and to whose leadership more recently Dion had been elected. The youths had heard what had occurred—that imprisonment, perhaps even worse disaster, threatened him. At any other time it would scarcely have been possible to oppose the decree of the Government and guard their imperilled friend, but in these dark days the rulers must deal with them. Though they were loyal to the Queen, and had resolved, spite of her defeat, to support her cause, as soon as she needed them, they would not suffer Dion to be punished for a crime which, in their eyes, was an honour. Their determination to protect him grew more eager with every vexatious delay on the part of the city council to deal with a matter which concerned one of their own body. They had not yet decided whether to demand a full pardon or only a mild sentence for the man who had wounded the "King of kings," the son of the sovereign. Moreover, the quiet Cæsarion, still subject to his tutor, had not understood how to win the favour of the Ephebi. The weakling never appeared in the Palæstra, which even the great Mark Antony did not disdain to visit. The latter had more than once given the youths assembled there proofs of his giant strength, and his son Antyllus also frequently shared their exercises. Dion had merely dealt Cæsarion with his clenched fist one of the blows which every one must encounter in the arena.

Philotas of Amphissa, the pupil of Didymus, had been the first to inform them of the attack and, with fiery zeal, had used his utmost power to atone for the wrong done to his master's granddaughter. His appeal had roused the most eager sympathy. The Ephebi believed themselves strong enough to defend their friend against any one and, if the worst should come, they knew they would be sustained by the council, the Exegetus, the captain of the guard—a brave Macedonian, who had once been an ornament of their own band—and the numerous clients of Dion and his family. There was not a single weakling among them. They had already found an opportunity to prove this; for, though they had arrived too late to protect Didymus's property from injury, they had checked the fury of the mob whose passions Philostratus had aroused, and forced back the crowd whom the Syrian led to Barine's dwelling to devote it to the same fate.

Another equipage was already standing before the door of Berenike's house—one of the carriages which were always at the disposal of the Queen's officials—when Anukis left Archibius's vehicle. Had some of Alexas's myrmidons arrived, or was he himself on the way to examine Dion, or even arrest him? The driver, like all the palace servants, knew Anukis, and she learned from him that he had brought Gorgias, the architect.

Anukis had never met the latter, though, during the rebuilding of Cæsarion's apartments, she had often seen him, and heard much of him; among other things, that Dion's beautiful palace was his work. He was a friend of the wounded man, so she need not fear him.

When she entered the atrium she heard that Berenike had gone out to drive with Archibius and his Roman friend. The leech had forbidden his patient to see many visitors. No one had been admitted except Gorgias and one of Dion's freedmen.

But time pressed; people of the same rank and disposition understand one another; the old porter and the Nubian were both loyal to their employers, and, moreover, were natives of the same country; so it required only a few words to persuade the door-keeper to conduct her without delay to the bedside of the wounded man.

The freedman, a tall, weather-beaten greybeard, simply clad, who looked like a pilot, was waiting outside the sick-room. He had not yet been admitted to Dion's presence, but this did not appear to vex him, for he stood leaning quietly against the wall beside the door, gazing at the broad-brimmed sailor's hat which he was slowly turning in his hands.

Scarcely had Dion heard Anukis's name, when an eager "Let her come in" reached her ears through the half-open door.

The Nubian waited to be summoned, but her dark face must have showed distinctly that something important and urgent had brought her here, for the wounded man added to his first words of greeting the expression of a fear that she had no good news.

Her reply was an eager nod of assent, accompanied by a doubtful glance at Gorgias; and Dion now curtly told the architect the name of the newcomer, and assured her that his friend might hear everything, even the greatest secret.

Anukis uttered a sigh of relief and then, in a tone of the most earnest warning, poured forth the story of the impending danger. She would not be satisfied when he spoke of the Ephebi, who were ready to defend him, and the council, which would make the cause of one of its members its own, but entreated him to seek some safe place of refuge, no matter where; for powers against whom no resistance would avail were stretching their hands towards him. Even this statement, however, proved useless, for Dion was convinced that the influence of his uncle, the Keeper of the Seal, would guard him from any serious danger. Then Anukis resolved to confess what she had overheard; but she told the story without mentioning Barine, and the peril threatening her also. Finally, with all the warmth of a really anxious heart, she entreated him to heed her warning.

Even while she was still speaking, the friends exchanged significant glances; but scarcely had the last words fallen from her lips when the giant figure of the freedman passed through the door, which had remained open.

"You here, Pyrrhus?" cried the wounded man kindly.

"Yes, master, it is I," replied the stalwart fellow, twirling his sailor hat still faster. "Listening isn't exactly my trade, and I don't usually enter your presence uninvited; but I couldn't help hearing what came through the door, and the croaking of the old raven drew me in."

"I wish you had heard more cheerful things," replied Dion; "but the brown-skinned bird of ill omen usually sings pleasant songs, and they all come from a faithful heart. But when my silent Pyrrhus opens his mouth so far, something important must surely follow, and you can speak freely in her presence."

The sailor cleared his throat, gripped his coarse felt hat in his sinewy hands, and said, in such a tremulous, embarrassed tone that his heavy chin quivered and his voice sometimes faltered: "If the woman is to be trusted, you must leave here, master, and seek some safe hiding-place. I came to offer one. On my way I heard your name. It was said that you had wounded the Queen's son, and it might cost you your life. Then I thought: 'No, no, not that, so long as Pyrrhus lives, who taught his young master Dion to use the oars and to set his first sail—Pyrrhus and his family.' Why repeat what we both know well enough? From my first boat and the land on our island to the liberty you bestowed upon us, we owe everything to your father and to you, and a blessing has rested upon your gift and our labour, and what is mine is yours. No more words are needed. You know our cliff beyond the Alveus Steganus, north of the great harbour—the Isle of Serpents. It is quickly gained by any one who knows the course through the water, but is as inaccessible to others as the moon and stars. People are afraid of the mere name, though we rid the island of the vermin long ago. My boys Dionysus, Dionichus, and Dionikus—they all have 'Dion' in their name—are waiting in the fish-market, and when it grows dusk——" Here the wounded man interrupted the speaker by holding out his hand and thanking him warmly for his fidelity and kindness, though he refused the well-meant invitation. He admitted that he knew no safer hiding-place than the cliff surrounded by fluttering sea-gulls, where Pyrrhus lived with his family and earned abundant support by fishing and serving as pilot. But anxiety concerning his future wife prevented his leaving the city.

The freedman however gave him no rest. He represented how quickly the harbour could be reached from his island, that fish were brought thence from it daily, and he would therefore always have news of what was passing. His sons were like him, and never used any unnecessary words; talking did not suit them. The women of the household rarely left the island. So long as it sheltered their beloved guest, they should not set foot away from it. If occasion should require, the master could be in Alexandria again quickly enough to put anything right.

This suggestion pleased the architect, who joined in the conversation to urge the freedman's request. But Dion, for Barine's sake, obstinately refused, until Anukis, who had long been anxious to go in pursuit of Archibius, thought it time to give *her* opinion.

"Go with the man, my lord!" she cried. "I know what I know. I will tell our Barine of your faithful resolution; but how can she show her gratitude for it if you are a dead man?"

This question and the information which followed it turned the scale; and, as soon as Dion had consented to accompany the freedman, the Nubian prepared to continue her errands, but the wounded man detained her to give many messages for Barine, and then she was stopped by the architect, who thought he had found in her the right assistant for numerous plans he had in his mind.

He had returned early that morning from Heroonpolis, where, with other members of his profession, he had inspected the newly constructed waterway. The result of the first investigation had been unfavourable to the verge of discouragement; and, in behalf of the others, he had gone to the Queen to persuade her to give up the enterprise which, though so full of promise, was impracticable in the short time at their disposal.

He had travelled all night, and was received as

soon as Cleopatra rose from her couch. He had driven from the Lochias in the carriage placed at his disposal because he had business at the arsenal and various points where building was going on, in order to inspect the wall erected for Antony on the Choma, and the Temple of Isis at the Corner of the Muses, to which Cleopatra desired to add a new building. But scarcely had he quitted the Bruchium when he was detained by the crowd assailing the house of Didymus with beams and rams, and at the same time keeping off the Ephebi who had attacked them.

He had forced his way through the raging mob to aid the old couple and their granddaughter. The slave Phryx had been busily preparing the boats which lay moored in the harbour of the sea-washed estate, but Gorgias had found it difficult to persuade the grey-haired philosopher to go with him and his family to the shore. He was ready to face the enraged rioters and—though it should cost his life—cry out that they were shamefully deceived and were staining themselves with a disgraceful crime. Not until the architect represented that it was unworthy of a Didymus to expose to bestial violence a life on which helpless women and the whole world—to whom his writings were guide-posts to the realms of truth—possessed a claim, could he be induced to yield. Nevertheless, the sage and his relatives almost fell into the hands of the furious rabble, for Didymus would not depart until he had saved this, that, and the other precious book, till the number reached twenty or thirty. Besides, his old deaf wife, who usually submitted quietly when her defective hearing prevented her comprehension of many things, insisted upon knowing what was occurring. She ordered everybody who came near her to explain what had happened, thus detaining her granddaughter Helena, who was trying to save the most valuable articles in the dwelling. So the departure was delayed, and only the brave defence of young Philotas, Didymus's assistant, and some of the Ephebi, who joined him, enabled them to escape unharmed.

The Scythian guards, which at last put a stop to the frantic rage of the deluded populace, arrived too late to prevent the destruction of the house, but they saved Philotas and the other youths from the fists and stones of the rabble.

When the boats had gone farther out into the harbour the question of finding a home for the philosopher and his family was discussed. Berenike's house was also threatened, and the rules of the museum prevented the reception of women. Five servants had accompanied the family, and none of Didymus's learned friends had room for so many guests. When the old man and Helena began to enumerate the lodgings of which they could think, Gorgias interposed with an entreaty that they would come to his house.

He had inherited the dwelling from his father. It was very large and spacious, almost empty, and they could reach it speedily, as it stood on the seashore, north of the Forum. The fugitives would be entirely at liberty there, since he had work on hand which would permit him to spend no time under his own roof except at night. He soon overcame the trivial objections made by the philosopher and, fifteen minutes after they had left the Corner of the Muses, he was permitted to open the door of his house to his guests, and he did so with genuine pleasure. The old housekeeper and the grey-haired steward, who had been in his father's service, looked surprised, but worked zealously after Gorgias had confided the visitors to their charge. The pressure of business forbade his fulfilling the duties of host in his own person.

Didymus and his family had reason to be grateful; and when the old sage found in the large library which the architect placed at his disposal many excellent books and among them some of his own, he ceased his restless pacing to and fro and forced himself to settle down. Then he remembered that, by the advice of a friend, he had placed his property in the keeping of a reliable banker and, though life still seemed dark grey, it no longer looked as black as before.

Gorgias briefly related all this to the Nubian, and Dion added that she would find Archibius with his Roman friend at the house of Berenike's brother, the philosopher Arius. Like himself, the latter was suffering from an injury inflicted by a reckless trick of Antyllus. Barine's mother was there also, so Anukis could inform them of the fate of Didymus and his brother, and tell them that he, Dion, intended to leave her house and the city an hour after sunset.

"But," interrupted Gorgias, "no one, not even your hostess Berenike and her brother, must know your destination.—You look as if you could keep a secret, woman."

"Though she owes her nickname Aisopion to her nimble tongue," replied Dion.

"But this tongue is like the little silver fish with scarlet spots in the palace garden," said Anukis. "They dart to and fro nimbly enough; but as soon as danger threatens they keep as quiet in the water as though they were nailed fast. And —by mighty Isis!—we have no lack of peril in these trying times. Would you like to see the lady Berenike and the others before your departure?"

"Berenike, yes; but the sons of Arius—they are fine fellows—would be wise to keep aloof from this house to-day."

"Yes indeed!" the architect chimed in. "It will be prudent for their father, too, to seek some hiding-place. He is too closely connected with Octavianus. It may indeed happen that the Queen will desire to make use of him. In that case he may be able to aid Barine, who is his sister's child.

Timagenes, too, who comes from Rome as a mediator, may have some influence."

"The same thoughts entered my poor brain also," said Anukis. "I am now going to show the gentlemen the danger which threatens her, and if I succeed—— Yet what could a serving-woman of my appearance accomplish? Still—my house is nearer to the brink of the stream than the dwelling of most others, and if I fling in a loaf, perhaps the current will bear it to the majestic sea."

"Wise Aisopion!" cried Dion; but the worthy maid-servant shrugged her crooked shoulders, saying: "We needn't be free-born to find pleasure in what is right; and if being wise means using one's brains to think, with the intention of promoting right and justice, you can always call me so. Then you will start after sundown?"

With these words she was about to leave the room, but the architect, who had watched her every movement, had formed a plan and begged her to follow him.

When they reached the next room he asked for a faithful account of Barine and the dangers threatening her. After consulting her as if she were an equal, he held out his hand in farewell, saying: "If it is possible to bring her to the Temple of Isis unseen, these clouds may scatter. I shall be in the sanctuary of the goddess from the first hour after sunset. I have some measurements to take there. When you say you know that the immortals will have pity on the innocent woman whom they have led to the verge of the abyss, perhaps you may be right. It seems as if matters here were combining in a way which would be apt to rob the story-teller of his listener's faith."

After Aisopion had gone, Gorgias returned to Dion's room and asked the freedman to be ready with his boat at a place on the shore which he carefully described.

The friends were again alone. Gorgias had his hands full of work, but he could not help expressing his surprise at the calm bearing which Dion maintained. "You behave as if you were going to an oyster supper at Kanopus," he said, shaking his head as though perplexed by some incomprehensible problem.

"What else would you have me do?" asked the Macedonian. "The vivid imagination of you artists shows you the future according to your own varying moods. If you hope, you transform a pleasant garden into the Elysian fields; if you fear anything, you behold in a burning roof the conflagration of a world. We, from whose cradle the Muse was absent, who use only sober reason to provide for the welfare of the household and the state, as well as for our own, see facts as they are and treat them like figures in a sum. I know that Barine is in danger. That might drive me frantic; but beyond her I see Archibius and Charmian spreading their protecting wings over her head; I perceive the fear of my faction, including the museum, of the council of which I am a member, of my clients and the conditions of the times, which precludes arousing the wrath of the citizens. The product which results from the correct addition of all these known quantities——"

"Will be correct," interrupted his friend, "so long as the most incalculable of all factors, passion, does not blend with them—the passion of a woman—and the Queen belongs to the sex which is certainly more powerful in that domain."

"Granted! But as soon as Mark Antony returns it will be proved that her jealousy was needless."

"We will hope so. It is only the misled, deceived, abused Cleopatra whom I fear; for she herself is matchless in divine goodness. The charm by which she ensnares hearts is indescribable, and the iron power of her intellect! I tell you, Dion——"

"Friend, friend," was the laughing interruption. "How high your wishes soar! For three years I have kept an account of the conflagrations in your heart. I believe we had reached seventeen; but this last one is equal to two."

"Folly!" cried Gorgias in an irritated tone. "May not a man admire what is magnificent, wonderful, unique? She is all these things! Just now —how long ago is it?—she appeared before me in a radiance of beauty——"

"Which should have made you shade both eyes. Yet you have been speaking so warmly of your young guest, her loving caution, her gentle calmness in the midst of peril——"

"Do you suppose I wish to recall a single syllable?" the architect indignantly broke in. "Helena has no peer among the maidens of Alexandria —but the other—Cleopatra—is elevated in her divine majesty above all ordinary mortals. You might spare me and yourself that scornful curl of the lip. Had she gazed into your face with those tearful, sorrowful eyes, as she did into mine, and spoken of her misery, you would have gone through fire and water, hand in hand with me, for her sake. I am not a man who is easily moved, and since my father's death the only tears I have seen have been shed by others; but when she talked of the mausoleum I was to build for her because Fate, she knew not how soon, might force her to seek refuge in the arms of death, my calmness vanished. Then, when she numbered me among the friends on whom she could rely and held out her hand—a matchless hand—oh! laugh if you choose— I felt I know not how, and kneeling at her feet I kissed it; it was wet with my tears. I am not ashamed of this emotion, and my lips seem consecrated since they touched the little white hand which spoke a language of its own and stands before my eyes wherever I gaze."

Pushing back his thick locks from his brow as

he spoke, he shook his head as though dissatisfied with himself and, in an altered tone, hurriedly continued: "But this is a time ill-suited for such ebullitions of feeling. I mentioned the mausoleum, whose erection the Queen desires. She will see the first hasty sketch to-morrow. It is already before my mind's eye. She wished to have it adjoin the Temple of Isis, her goddess—— I proposed the great sanctuary in the Rhakotis quarter, but she objected—she wished to have it close to the palace at Lochias. She had thought of the temple at the Corner of the Muses, but the house occupied by Didymus stood in the way of a larger structure. If this were removed it would be possible to carry the street through the old man's garden, perhaps even to the sea-shore, and we should have had space for a gigantic edifice and still left room for a fine garden. But we had learned how the philosopher loved his family estate. The Queen is unwilling to use violence towards the old man—— She is just, and perhaps other reasons, of which I am ignorant, influence her. So I promised to look for another site, though I saw how much she desired to have her tomb connected with the sanctuary of her favourite goddess—— Then—I have already told the clever brown witch—then the immortals, Divinity, Fate, or whatever we call the power which guides the world and our lives according to eternal laws and its own mysterious, omnipotent will, permitted a rascally deed, from which I think may come deliverance for you and a source of pleasure to the Queen in these days of trial."

"Man, man! Where will this new passion lead you? The horses are stamping impatiently outside; duty summons the most faithful of men, and he stands like a prophet, indulging in mysterious sayings!"

"Whose meaning and purport, spite of your calm calculations of existing circumstances, will soon seem no less wonderful to you than to me, whose unruly artist nature, according to your opinion, is playing me a trick," retorted the architect. "Now listen to this explanation: Didymus's house will be occupied at once by my workmen, but I shall examine the lower rooms of the Temple of Isis. I have with me a document requiring obedience to my orders. Cleopatra herself laid the plans before me, even the secret portion showing the course of the subterranean chambers. It will cast some light upon my mysterious sayings if I bear you away from the enemy through one of the secret corridors. They were right in concealing from you by how slender a thread, spite of the power of your example in mathematics, the sword hangs above your head. Now that I see a possibility of removing it, I can show it to you. To-morrow you would have fallen, without hope of rescue, into the hands of cruel foes and been shamefully abandoned by your own weak uncle, had not the most implacable of all your enemies permitted himself the infamous pleasure of laying hands on an old man's house, and the Queen, in consequence of an agitating message, had the idea suggested of building her own mausoleum. The corridor "—here he lowered his voice—" of which I spoke leads to the sea at a spot close beside Didymus's garden, and through it I will guide you, and, if possible, Barine also, to the shore. This could be accomplished in the usual way only by the greatest risk. If we use the passage we can reach a dark place on the strand unseen, and unless some special misfortune pursues us our flight will be unnoticed. The litters and your tottering gait would betray everything if we were to enter the boat anywhere else in the great harbour."

"And we, sensible folk, refuse to believe in miracles!" cried Dion, holding out his wan hand to the architect. "How shall I thank you, you dear, clever, most loyal of friends to your male friends, though your heart is so faithless to fair ones? Add that malicious speech to the former ones, for which I now crave your pardon. What you intend to accomplish for Barine and me gives you a right to do and say to me whatever ill you choose all the rest of my life. Anxiety for her would surely have bound me to this house and the city when the time came to make the escape, for without her my life would now be valueless. But when I think that she might follow me to Pyrrhus's cliff——"

"Don't flatter yourself with this hope," pleaded Gorgias. "Serious obstacles may interpose. I am to have another talk with the Nubian later. With no offence to others, I believe her advice will be the best. She knows how matters stand with the lofty, and yet herself belongs to the lowly. Besides, through Charmian the way to the Queen lies open, and nothing which happens at court escapes her notice. She showed me that we must consider Barine's delivery to Alexas a piece of good fortune. How easily jealousy might have led to a fatal crime one whose wish promptly becomes action, unless she curbs the undue zeal of her living tools! Those on whom Fate inflicts so many blows rarely are in haste to spare others. Would the anxieties which weigh upon her like mountains interpose between the Queen and the jealous rancour which is too petty for her great soul?"

"What is great or petty to the heart of a loving woman?" asked Dion. "In any case you will do what you can to remove Barine from the power of the enraged princess—I know."

Gorgias pressed his friend's hand closely, then, yielding to a sudden impulse, kissed him on the forehead and hurried to the door.

On the threshold a faint moan from the wounded man stopped him. Would he be strong enough to follow the long passage leading to the sea?

Dion protested that he confidently expected to

do so, but his deeply flushed face betrayed that the fever which had once been conquered had returned.

Gorgias's eyes sought the floor in deep thought. Many sick persons were borne to the temple in the hope of cure; so Dion's appearance would cause no special surprise. On the other hand, to have strangers carry him through the passage seemed perilous. He himself was strong, but even the strongest person would have found it impossible to support the heavy burden of a grown man to the sea, for the gallery was low and of considerable length. Still, if necessary, he would try. With the comforting exclamation, "If your strength does not suffice, another way will be found," he took his leave, gave Barine's maid and the wounded man's body-slave the necessary directions, commanded the door-keeper to admit no one save the physician, and stepped into the open air.

A little band of Ephebi were pacing to and fro before the house. Others had flung themselves down in an open space surrounded by shrubbery in the Paneum garden, and were drinking the choice wine which Dion's cellarer, by his orders, had brought and was pouring out for the crowd.

It was an animated scene, for the clients of the sufferer, who, after expressing their sympathy, had been dismissed by the porter, and bedizened girls had joined the youths. There was no lack of jests and laughter, and when some pretty young mother or female slave passed by leading children, with whom the garden was a favourite playground, many a merry word was exchanged.

Gorgias waved his hands gaily to the youths, pleased with the cheerfulness with which the brave fellows transformed duty into a festival, and many raised their wine-cups, shouting a joyous "Io" and "Evoe," to drink the health of the famous artist who not long ago had been one of themselves.

The others were led by a slender youth, the student Philotas, from Amphissa, Didymus's assistant, whom the architect, a few days before, had helped to liberate from the demons of wine. Even while Gorgias was beckoning to him from the two-wheeled chariot, the thought entered his mind that yonder handsome youth, who had so deeply wronged Barine and Dion, would be the very person to help carry his friend through the low-roofed passage to the sea. If Philotas was the person Gorgias believed him to be, he would deem it a special favour to make amends for his crime to those whom he had injured, and he was not mistaken; for, after the youth had taken a solemn oath not to betray the secret to any one, the architect asked him to aid in Dion's rescue. Philotas, overflowing with joyful gratitude, protested his willingness to do so, and promised to wait at the appointed spot in the Temple of Isis at the time mentioned.

CHAPTER XIV.

WHILE Gorgias was examining the subterranean chambers in the Temple of Isis, Charmian returned to Lochias earlier than she herself had expected. She had met her brother, whom she did not find at Kanopus, at Berenike's, and after greeting Dion on his couch of pain, she told Archibius of her anxiety. She confided to him alone that the Queen had committed Barine's fate to Alexas, for the news might easily have led the mother of the endangered woman to some desperate venture; but even Archibius's composure, so difficult to disturb, was not proof against it. He would have sought the Queen's presence at once—if necessary, forced his way to it; but the historian Timagenes, who had just come from Rome, was expecting him, and he had not returned to his birthplace as a private citizen, but commissioned by Octavianus to act as mediator in putting an end to the struggle which had really been decided in his favour at the battle of Actium. The choice of this mediator was a happy one; for he had taught Cleopatra in her childhood, and was the self-same quick-witted man who had so often roused her to argument. His share in a popular insurrection against the Roman rule had led to his being carried as a slave to the Tiber. There he soon purchased his freedom, and attained such distinction that Octavianus entrusted this important mission to the man who was so well known in Alexandria. Archibius was to meet him at the house of Arius, who was still suffering from the wounds inflicted by the chariot-wheels of Antyllus, and Berenike had accompanied Timagenes to her brother.

Charmian did not venture to go there; a visit to Octavianus's former teacher would have been misinterpreted, and it was repugnant to her own delicacy of feeling to hold intercourse at this time with the foe and conqueror of her royal mistress.

She therefore let her brother drive with Berenike to the injured man's; but before his departure Archibius had promised, if the worst came, to dare everything to open the eyes of the Queen, who had forbidden her, Charmian, to speak in behalf of Barine and thwart the plans of Alexas.

From the Paneum garden she was carried to the Kanopic Way and the Jewish quarter, where she had many important purchases to make for Cleopatra. It was long after noon when the litter was again borne to Lochias.

On the way she had severely felt her own powerlessness. Without having accomplished anything herself, she was forced to wait for the success of others; and she had scarcely crossed the threshold of the palace ere fresh cares were added to those which already burdened her soul.

She understood how to read the faces of courtiers, and the door-keeper's had taught her that since her departure something momentous had occurred. She disliked to question the slaves and lower officials, so she refrained, though the interior of the palace was crowded with guards, officials of every grade, attendants, and slaves. Many who saw her gazed at her with the timidity inspired by those over whom some disaster is impending. Others, whose relations were more intimate, pressed forward to enjoy the mournful satisfaction of being the first messengers of evil tidings. But she passed swiftly on, keeping them back with grave words and gestures, until, before the door of the great anteroom thronged with Greek and Egyptian petitioners, she met Zeno, the Keeper of the Seal. Charmian stopped him and inquired what had happened.

"Since when?" asked the old courtier. "Every moment has brought some fresh tidings and all are mournful. What terrible times, Charmian, what disasters!"

"No messenger had arrived when I left the Lochias," replied Charmian. "Now it seems as though the old monster of a palace, accustomed to so many horrors, is holding its breath in dread.

Tell me the main thing, at least, before I meet the Queen."

"The main thing? Pestilence or famine—which shall we call the worse?"

"Quick, Zeno! I am expected."

"I, too, am in haste, and really there is nothing to relate over which the tongue would care to dwell. Candidus arrived first. Came himself straight from Actium. The fellow is bold enough."

"Is the army defeated also?"

"Defeated, dispersed, deserted to the foe—King Herod with his legions in the van."

Charmian covered her face with her hands and groaned aloud, but Zeno continued:

"You were with her in the flight. When Mark Antony left you, he sailed with the ships which joined him for Parætonium. A large body of troops on which the Queen and Mardion had fixed their hopes was encamped there. Reinforcements could easily be gained and we should once more have a fine army at our disposal."

"Pinarius Scarpus, a cautious soldier, was in command; and I, too, believed——"

"The more you trusted him, the greater would be your error. The shameless rascal—he owes everything to Antony—had received tidings of Actium ere the ships arrived, and had already made overtures to Octavianus when the Imperator came. The veterans who opposed the treachery were hewn down by the wretch's orders, but the brave garrison of the city could not be won over to the monstrous crime. It is due to these men that Mark Antony still lives and did not come to a miserable end at the hands of his own troops. The twice-defeated general—a courier brought the news—will arrive to-night. Strangely enough, he will not come to Lochias, but to the little palace on the Choma."

"Poor, poor Queen!" cried Charmian; "how did she bear all this?"

"In the presence of the defeated Candidus and Antony's messenger like a heroine. But afterwards —— Her raving did not last long; but the mute, despairing silence!—— Ere she had fully recovered her self-command she sent us all away, and I have not seen her since. But all the thoughts and feelings which dwell here"—he pointed to his brow and breast —"have left their abode and linger with her. I totter from place to place like a soulless body. O Charmian! what has befallen us? Where are the days when care and trouble lay buried with the other dead —the days and nights when my brain united with that of the Queen to transform this desolate earth into the beautiful Elysian Fields, every-day life to a festival, festivals to the very air of Olympus? What unprecedented scenes of splendour had I not devised for the celebration of the victory, the triumph—nay, even the entry into Rome! Whole chests are filled with the sketches, programmes, drawings, and verses. All who handle brush and chisel, compose and execute music, would have lent their aid, and—you may believe me—the result would have been something which future generations would have discussed, lauded, and extolled in song. And now—now?"

"Now we will double our efforts to save what is yet to be rescued!"

"Rescued?" repeated the courtier in a hollow tone. "The Queen, too, still clings to this fine word. When I saw her at work yesterday, it seemed as if I beheld her drawing water with the bottomless vessel of the Danaides. True, to-day, when I left her, her arms had fallen—and in this attitude she now stands before me with her tearful eyes. And besides, I can't get my nephew Dion out of my mind. Cares—nothing but cares concerning him! And my intentions towards him were so kind! My will gives him my entire fortune; but now he actually wants to marry the singer, the daughter of the artist Leonax. You have taken her under your protection, but surely your own niece, Iras, is dearer to you, so you will approve of my destroying the will if Dion insists upon his own way. He shall not have a solidus of my property if he does not give up the woman who is a thorn in the Queen's flesh. And his choice does not suit our ancient race. Iras, on the contrary, was Dion's playfellow, and I have long destined her for his wife. No better match, nor one more acceptable to the Queen, could be found for him. He cared for her until the singer bewitched him. Bring them together, and they shall be like my own children. If the fool resists his uncle, whose sole desire is to benefit him, I will withdraw my aid. Whatever intrigues his foes may weave, I shall fold my arms and not interfere. I stand in the place of his father, my dead brother, and demand obedience. The Queen is my universe, and her favour is of more value than twenty refractory nephews."

"You will retain her Majesty's favour, even if you intercede for your brother's son."

"And Iras? When she finds herself deceived—and she will soon discover it—she will not rest——"

"Until she has brought ruin upon him," interrupted Charmian, in a tone of sorrow rather than reproach as though she already beheld the impending disaster. "But Iras has no greater influence with the Queen than I, and if you and I unite to protect the brave young fellow, who is of your own blood——"

"Then, of course—no doubt, on account of your longer period of service, you have more influence with her Majesty than Iras—however—such matters must be considered—and I have already said—my mind leaves its abode to follow the Queen like her shadow. It heeds only what concerns her. Let everything else go as it will. The fleet the same as destroyed, Candidus defeated, Herod a deserter, treason on treason—the African legions lost! What in the name of the god who tried to roll back the wheel dashing down the mountain-side!—— And yet! Let us offer sacrifices, my friend, and hope for better days!"

Zeno retired as he spoke, but Charmian moved forward with a drooping head to find Barine and her faithful Anukis, and weep her fill ere she went to perform the duty of consoling and sustaining her beloved mistress. Yet she herself so sorely needed comfort. Wherever she turned her eyes she beheld disaster, peril, treachery, and base intrigues. She felt as if she had lived long enough, and that her day was over. Hitherto her gentle nature, her intellect, which yearned to expand, gather new riches, and exchange what it had gained with others, had possessed much to offer to the Queen. She had not only been Cleopatra's confidante, but necessary to her to discuss questions far in advance of the demands of the times, which occupied her restless mind. Now the Queen's attention was wholly absorbed by events—hard, cruel facts—which she must resist or turn to her own advantage. Her life had become a conflict, and Charmian felt that she was by no means combative. The hard, supple, keenly polished intellect of Iras now asserted its value, and the elderly woman told herself that she was in danger of being held in less regard than her younger companion. To resign her office would have given her peace of mind, but she repelled the thought. For the very reason that these days were so full of misery and perhaps drawing nearer to the end, she must remain, first for the sake of the Queen, but also to watch over Barine.

Now she longed to go to Cleopatra. Her mere presence, she knew, would do her sore heart good.

The silvery laugh of a child reached her ears through the open gate of the garden which she was rapidly approaching. Little six-year-old Alexander ran towards her with open arms, hugged her closely, pressed his curly head against her, and gazed into her face with his large clear eyes.

Charmian's heart swelled; and as she raised the child in her arms and kissed him, she thought of the sad fate impending, and the composure maintained with so much difficulty gave way; tears streamed from her eyes and, sobbing violently, she pressed the boy closer to her breast.

The prince, accustomed to bright faces and tender caresses, broke away from her in terror to run back to his brother and sisters. But he had a kind little heart, and, knowing that no one weeps and sobs unless in pain, Alexander pitied Charmian, whom he loved, and hurried to her again.

What he meant to show her had pleased his mother, too, and dried the tears in her eyes. So he took Charmian by the hand and drew her along, saying that he wanted her to see the prettiest thing. She willingly allowed herself to be led over the paths, strewn with red sand, of the little garden which Antony had had laid out for his children in the magnificent style which pleased his love of splendour, and filled with rare and beautiful things.

There was a pond with tiny gold and silver fish, where the rare lotus flowers with pink blossoms arose from amid their smooth green leaves, and another where dwarf ducks of every colour, which seemed as if they had been created for children, swam to and fro. A bit of the sea which washed its shore had been enclosed by a gilded lattice-work, and on its surface floated a number of snow-white swans and black ones with scarlet bills. Native and Indian flowers of every hue adorned the beds, and the narrow paths were shaded by arbours made of gold wire, over which ran climbing vines filled with bright blossoms.

A grotto of stalactites behind the dense foliage of an Indian tree offered a resting-place, and beside it was a little house where the children could stay. The interior lacked none of the requisites of living, not even the cooking utensils in the kitchen, and the family portraits in the tablinum, delicately painted by an artist on small ivory slabs. Everything was made to suit the size of children, but of the most costly material and careful workmanship.

Behind the house was a little stable where four tiny horses with spotted skins, the rarest and prettiest creatures imaginable—a gift from the King of Media—were stamping the ground.

In another place was an enclosure containing gazelles, ostriches, young giraffes, and other grass-eating animals. Bright-plumaged birds and monkeys filled the tops of the trees, gay balls rose and fell on the jets of the fountains, and child genii and images of the gods in bronze and marble peered from the foliage. This whole enchanted world was comprised within a narrow space, and, with its radiance of colour and wealth of form, its perfume, songs, and warbling, exerted a bewildering influence upon the excited imaginations of grown people as well as children.

Little Alexander, without even casting a glance at all this, drew Charmian forward. He did not pause until he reached the shore of the lotus pond; then, putting his fingers on his lips, he said: "There, now, I'll show you. Look here!"

Rising cautiously upon tip-toe as he spoke, he pointed to the hollow in the trunk of a tree. A pair of finches had built their nest in it, and five young ones with big yellow beaks stretched their ugly little heads hungrily upward.

"That's so pretty!" cried the prince. "And you must see the old ones come to feed them."

The beautiful boy's sweet face fairly beamed with delight, and Charmian kissed him tenderly. Yet, even as she did so, she thought of the young swallows hacked to death in his mother's galley, and a chill ran through her veins.

Just at that moment voices were heard calling

Alexander from a neglected spot behind the dainty little house built for the children, and the boy exclaimed peevishly:

"There, now, I showed you the little nest, so I forgot. Agatha fell asleep and Smerdis went away, so we were alone. Then they sent me to Horus, the gate-keeper, to get some of his spelt bread. He never says no to anything, and it does taste so good. We're peasants, and have been using the axe and the hoe, so we want something to eat. Have you seen our house? We built it ourselves. Selene, Helios, Jotape, my future wife, and I—yes, I! They let me help, and we finished it alone, all alone! Everything is here. We shall build the shed for the cow to-morrow. The others mustn't see it, but I may show it to you."

While speaking, he drew her forward again, and Charmian obediently followed. The twins and little Jotape, who had been chosen for the future bride of the six-year-old Prince Alexander— a pretty, delicate, fair-haired child of his own age, the daughter of the Median king, who had been betrothed to the boy after the Parthian war, and now remained as a hostage at Cleopatra's court— welcomed her with joyous shouts. With the exception of the little Median princess, Charmian had witnessed their birth, and they all loved her dearly.

The little royal labourers showed their work with proud delight, and it really was well done.

They had toiled at it for weeks, paying no heed to the garden and all its costly rarities. They pointed with special pride to the two planks which Helios, aided by Alexander, had fished out of the sea after the last storm, when they were left alone, and to the lock on the door which they had secretly managed to wrench from an old gate. Selene herself had woven the curtain in front of the door. Now they were going to build a hearth too.

Charmian praised their skill, while they—all talking merrily together—told her how they had conquered the greatest difficulties. Their bright eyes sparkled with pleasure while describing the work of their own hands, and they were so absorbed in eager delight that they did not notice the approach of a man until startled by his words: "Enough of this idle sport now, your Highnesses. Too much time has already been wasted on it."

Then, turning to the Queen, who had accompanied him, he continued in a tone of apology: "This amusement might seem somewhat hazardous, yet there is much to be said in its favour. Besides, it appeared to afford the royal children so much pleasure that I permitted it for a short time. But if your Majesty commands——"

"Let them have their pleasure," the Queen interrupted kindly; and as soon as the children saw their mother they rushed forward, crowded around her with fearless love, thanked her, and eagerly assured her that nothing in the whole garden was half so dear to them as their little house. They meant to build a stable too.

"That might be too much," said the tutor Euphronion, a grey-haired man with a shrewd, kindly face. "We must remember how many things are yet to be learned, that we may reach the goal fixed for your Majesty's birthday and pass the examination."

But all the children now joined in the entreaty to be allowed to build the stable too, and it was granted.

When the tutor at last began to lead them away, the royal mother stopped them, asking:

"Suppose, instead of this garden, I should give you a bit of bare land, such as the peasants till, where, after your lessons, you might dig and build as much as you please?"

Loud shouts of joy from the children answered the question; but the little Median girl, Jotape, said hesitatingly:

"Could I take my doll too—only the oldest, Atossa? She has lost one arm, yet I love her the best."

"Deprive us of anything you choose!" cried Helios, drawing little Alexander towards him, to show that they, the men, were of the same mind, "only give us some ground and let us build."

"We will consider whether it can be done," replied Cleopatra. "Perhaps, Euphronion, you would be the right person—— But we will discuss the matter at a more quiet hour."

The tutor withdrew and the children, who followed, looked back, waving their hands and calling to their mother for a long time.

When they had disappeared behind the shrubbery in the garden Charmian exclaimed, "However dark the sky may be, so long as you possess these little ones you can never lack sunshine."

"If," replied Cleopatra, gazing pensively at the ground, "with a thought of them another did not blend which makes the gloom become deeper still. You know the tidings this terrible day has brought?"

"All," replied Charmian, sighing heavily.

"Then you know the abyss on whose verge we are walking; and to see them—them also dragged into the yawning gulf by their unhappy mother—O Charmian, Charmian!"

She sobbed aloud, threw her arms around the neck of her friend and playfellow, and laid her head upon her bosom like a child seeking consolation. Cleopatra wept for several minutes, and when she again raised her tear-stained face she said softly:

"That did me good! O, Charmian! no one needs love as I do. On your warm heart my own has already grown calmer."

"Use it, nestle there whenever you need it, to the end," cried Charmian, deeply moved.

"To the end," repeated Cleopatra, wiping her eyes. "It began to-day, I think. I have just spent an hour alone. I meant to commit a crime, and you know how impatiently passion sweeps me along. But what misfortunes have assailed me! The army destroyed; the desertion of Herod and Pinarius; Antony's generous, trusting heart torn by base treachery, his soul darkened; the reconstruction of the canal, the last hope—Gorgias brought the news—the same as destroyed. Just then little Alexander came to show me his bird's nest. Everything else in the garden seemed to him worthless by comparison. This awakened new thoughts, and now here is the little house which the children have built with their own hands. All these things forced me by some mysterious power to look back along the course of my life to the distant days in your father's house—I—— These children! Upon what different foundations our lives have been built! I made them begin at the point I had gained when youth lay behind me. *My* childhood commenced among the disorders of the government, clouded by my father's exile and my mother's death, on the brink of ruin. That of the twins—they are ten years old—will soon be over—and now, after enjoying pleasures not one of which was bestowed on me, they must endure the same sorrow. But did not we have better ones? What they daily possessed we only dreamed of in our simple garden. How often I let you share the radiant visions which my soul revealed to me! You willingly accompanied me into the splendid fairy world of my dreams. All that my imagination conjured up during the years of quiet and repose accompanied me into my after-life. Again and again I have beheld them, rich and powerful, upon the throne. The means of rendering the vision a verity were at hand; and when I met the man whose own life resembled the realization of a dream, I recalled those childish fancies and made them facts. The marvels with which I adorned my lover's existence were childish dreams to which I gave tangible form. This garden is an image of the life to which I intended to rise; in reality, fell. We collected within the limits of this bit of earth everything which can delight the senses; not a single one is omitted in this narrow space, whose crowded maze of pleasures fairly impede freedom of movement. Yet in your home, and guided by your wise father, I had learned to be content with so little, and commenced the struggle to attain peace. That painless peace—our chief good—whence came it? Through me it was lost to you both—— But the children—I made them begin their lives in an arena of every disturbing influence; and now I see how their own healthy natures yearn to escape from the dazzling wealth of colour, the stupefying fragrance, the bewildering songs and twittering. They long to return to the untilled earth, where the life of struggling mortals began.

The boy casts away the baubles, to test his own creative powers. The girl follows his example, and clings fast only to the doll in which she sees the living child, in order to do justice to the maternal instinct, the token of her sex. But what they so eagerly desire is right, and shall be granted. When I was ten years old, like the twins, my life and efforts were already directed towards one fixed goal. They are still blindly following the objects set before them. Let them return to the place whence their mother started, where she received everything good which is still hers. They shall go to the garden of Epicurus, no matter whether it is the old one in Kanopus or elsewhere. All that their mother beheld in vivid dreams, which she often strove with wanton extravagance to realize, has surrounded them from their birth and early satiated them. When they enter life, they will scorn what merely stirs and dazzles the senses, and cling to the aspiration for painless peace of mind, if a wise guide directs them and protects them from the dangers which the teachings of Epicurus contain for youth. I have found this guide, and you, too, will trust him—I mean your brother Archibius."

"Archibius?" asked Charmian in surprise.

"Yes, he who grew up in the garden of Epicurus, and in life and philosophy found the support which has preserved his peace of mind during all the conflicts of existence—he who loves the mother, and to whom the children are also dear—

he to whom the boys and girls cling with affectionate confidence. I wish to place the children under his protection and, if he will consent to grant this desire of the most hapless of women, I shall look forward calmly to the end. It is approaching! I feel, I know it! Gorgias is already at work upon the plan for my tomb."

"O my Queen!" cried Charmian sorrowfully. "Whatever may happen, your illustrious life cannot be in danger! The generous heart of Mark Antony does not throb in Octavianus's breast, but he is not cruel, and for the very reason that cool calculation curbs ambition he will spare you. He knows that you are the idol of the city, the whole country; and if he really succeeds in adding fresh victories to this first conquest, if the immortals permit your throne and—may they avert it!—your sacred person, too, to fall into his power——"

"Then," cried Cleopatra, her clear eyes flashing, "then he shall learn which of us two is the greater—then I shall know how to maintain the right to despise him, though blind Fate should make the whole power of the world subject to him who robbed my son and Cæsar's of his heritage!"

Her eyes had blazed with anger as she uttered the words; then, letting her little clenched hand fall, she went on in an altered tone:

"Months may pass before he is strong enough to risk the attack, and the immortals themselves approved the erection of the monument. The only obstacle in the way, the house of the old philosopher Didymus, was destroyed. A messenger from Gorgias brought the news. It is to be the second monument in Alexandria worthy of notice. The other contains the body of the great Alexander, to whom the city owes its origin and name. He who subjected half the world to his power and the genius of the Greeks, was younger than I when he died. Whence do I, by whose miserable weakness the battle of Actium was lost, derive the right to walk longer beneath the sun? Perhaps Mark Antony will arrive in a few hours."

"And will you meet the disheartened hero in this mood?" interrupted Charmian.

"He does not wish to be received," answered Cleopatra bitterly. "He even refused to let me greet him, and I understand the denial. But what must have overwhelmed this joyous nature, so friendly to all mankind, that he longs for solitude and avoids meeting those who are nearest and dearest? Iras is now at the Choma—whither he wishes to retire—to see that everything is in order. She will also provide a supply of the flowers he loves. It is hard, cruelly hard, not to welcome him as usual. O Charmian, what joy it was when, with open arms and overflowing heart, he swung his mighty figure ashore like a youth, while his handsome, heroic face beamed with ardent love for me! And then—you do not forget it either—when he raised his deep voice to shout the first greeting, why, it seemed as if the very fish in the water must join in, and the palm-trees on the shore wave their feathery tops in joyous sympathy. And here! The dreams of my childhood, which I made reality for him, received us, and our existence, wreathed with love and roses, became a fairy tale. Since the day he rode towards us at Kanopus and offered me the first bouquet, with his sunny glance wooing my love, his image has stood before my soul as the embodiment of the virile strength which conquers everything, and the bright, undimmed joy which renders the whole world happy. And now—now? Do you remember the dull dreamer whom we left ere he set forth for Parætonium? But no, no, a thousand times no, he must not remain so! Not with bowed head, but erect as in the days of happiness, must he cross the threshold of Hades, hand in hand with her whom he loved. And he does love me still. Else would he have followed me hither, though no magic goblet drew him after me? And I? The heart which, in the breast of the child, gave him its first young love, is still his, and will be forever. Might I not go to the harbour and await him there? Look me in the face, Charmian, and answer me as fearlessly as a mirror: did Olympus really succeed in effacing the wrinkles?"

"They were scarcely visible before," was the reply, "and even the keenest eye could no longer discover them. I have brought the pomade, too, and the prescription Olympus gave me for——"

"Hush, hush!" interrupted Cleopatra softly. "There are many living creatures in this garden, and they say that even the birds are good listeners."

A roguish smile deepened the dimples in her cheeks as she spoke, and delight in her bewitching grace forced from Charmian's lips the exclamation:

"If Mark Antony could only see you now!"

"Flatterer!" replied the Queen with a grateful smile. But Charmian felt that the time had now come to plead once more for Barine, and she began eagerly:

"No, I certainly do not flatter. No one in Alexandria, no matter what name she bears, could venture to vie even remotely with your charms. So cease the persecution of the unfortunate woman whom you confided to my care. It is an insult to Cleopatra——"

But here an indignant "Again!" interrupted her.

Cleopatra's face, which during the conversation had mirrored every emotion of a woman's soul, from the deepest sorrow to the most mischievous mirth, assumed an expression of repellent harshness, and, with the curt remark, "You are forgetting what I had good reason to forbid— I must go to my work," she turned her back upon the companion of her youth.

CHAPTER XV.

CHARMIAN went towards her own apartments. How often she had had a similar experience! In the midst of the warmest admiration for this rare woman's depth of feeling, masculine strength of intellect, tireless industry, watchful care for her native land, steadfast loyalty, and maternal devotion, she had been sobered in the most pitiable way.

She had been forced to see Cleopatra, for the sake of realizing a childish dream, and impressing her lover, squander vast sums, which diminished the prosperity of her subjects; place great and important matters below the vain, punctilious care of her own person; forget, in petty jealousy, the justice and kindness which were marked traits in her character; and, though the most kindly and womanly of sovereigns, suffer herself to be urged by angry excitement to inflict outrage on a subject whose acts had awakened her displeasure. The lofty ambition which had inspired her noblest and most praiseworthy deeds had more than once been the source of acts which she herself regretted. When a child, she could not endure to be surpassed in difficult tasks, and still deemed it a necessity to be first and peerless. Hence the unfortunate circumstance that Antony had given Barine the counterpart of an armlet which she herself wore as a gift from her lover, was perhaps the principal cause of her bitter resentment against the hapless woman.

Charmian had seen Cleopatra forgive freely and generously many a wrong, nay, many an affront, inflicted upon her; but to see herself placed by her husband on the same plane as a Barine, even in the most trivial matter, might easily seem to her an unbearable insult; and the mishap which had befallen Cæsarion, in consequence of his foolish passion for the young beauty, gave her a right to punish her rival.

Deeply anxious concerning the fate of the woman in her care—greatly agitated, moreover, and exhausted physically and mentally—Charmian sought her own apartments.

Here she hoped to find solace in Barine's cheerful and equable nature; here the helpful hands of her dark-skinned maid and confidante awaited her.

The sun was low in the western horizon when she entered the anteroom. The members of the body-guard who were on duty told her that nothing unusual had occurred, and with a sigh of relief she passed into the sitting-room.

But the Ethiopian, who usually came to meet

her with words of welcome, took her veil and wraps, and removed her shoes, was absent. To-day no one greeted her. Not until she entered the second room, which she had assigned to her guest, did she find Barine, who was weeping bitterly.

During Charmian's absence the latter had received a letter from Alexas, in which he informed her that he was ordered by the Queen to subject her to an examination the next morning. Her cause looked dark but, if she did not render his duty harder by the harshness which had formerly caused him much pain, he would do his utmost to protect her from imprisonment, forced labour in the mines, or even worse misfortunes. The imprudent game which she had played with King Cæsarion had unfortunately roused the people against her. The depth of their indignation was shown by the fury with which they had assailed the house of her grandfather, Didymus. Nothing could save Dion, who had audaciously attacked the illustrious son of their beloved Queen, from the rage of the populace. He, Alexas, knew that in this Dion she would lose a friend and protector, but he would be disposed to take his place if her conduct did not render it impossible for him to unite mercy with justice.

This shameful letter, which promised Barine clemency in return for her favour without unmasking him in his character of judge, explained to Charmian the agitation in which she found her friend's daughter.

It was doubtless a little relief to Barine to express her loathing and abhorrence of Alexas as eagerly as her gentle nature would permit, but fear, grief, and indignation continued to struggle for the mastery in her oppressed soul.

It would have been expected that the keen-witted woman would have eagerly inquired what Charmian had accomplished with the Queen and Archibius, and what new events had happened to affect Cleopatra, the state, and the city; but she questioned her with far deeper interest concerning the welfare of her lover, desiring information in regard to many things of which her friend could give no tidings. In her brief visit to Dion's couch she had not learned how he bore his own misfortunes and Barine's, what view he took of the future, or what he expected from the woman he loved.

Charmian's ignorance and silence in regard to these very matters increased the anxiety of the endangered woman, who saw not only her own life, but those dearest to her, seriously threatened. So she entreated her hostess to relieve her from the uncertainty which was harder to endure than the most terrible reality; but the latter either could not or would not give her any further details of Cleopatra's intentions, or the fate and present abode of her grandparents and Helena. This increased her anxiety, for if Alexas's information was correct, her family must be homeless. When Charmian at last admitted that she had seen Dion only a few minutes, the tortured Barine's power of quiet endurance gave way.

She, whose nature was so hopeful that, when the glow of the sunset faded, she already anticipated with delight the rosy dawn of the next day, now beheld in Cleopatra's hand the reed which was to sign the death-sentence of Dion and herself. Her mental vision conjured up her relatives wounded by the falling house or bleeding under the stones hurled by the raging populace. She heard Alexas command the executioner to subject her to the rack, and fancied that Anukis had not returned because she had failed to find Dion. The Queen's soldiers had probably carried him to prison, loaded with chains, if Philostratus had not already instigated the mob to drag him through the streets.

With feverish impetuosity, which alarmed Charmian the more because it was so unlike her old friend's daughter, Barine described all the spectres with which her imagination—agitated by terror, longing, love, and loathing—terrified her; but the former exerted all the power of eloquence she possessed, by turns reproving her and loading her with caresses, in order to soothe her and rouse her from her despair. But nothing availed. At last she succeeded in persuading the unhappy woman to go with her to the window, which afforded a most beautiful view. Westward, beyond the Heptastadium, the sun was sinking below the forests of masts in the harbour of the Eunostus; and Charmian, who had learned from her intercourse with the royal children how to soothe a troubled young heart, to divert Barine's thoughts, directed her attention to the crimson glow in the western sky, and told her how her father, the artist, had showed her the superb brilliancy which colours gained at this hour of the day, even when the west was less radiant than now. But Barine, who usually could never gaze her fill at such a spectacle, did not thank her, for this sunset reminded her of another which she had lately watched at Dion's side, and she again broke into convulsive sobs.

Charmian, not knowing what to do, passed her arm around her. Just at that moment the door was hurriedly thrown open, and Anukis, the Nubian, entered.

Her mistress knew that something unusual must have happened to detain her so long from her post at Barine's side, and her appearance showed that she had been attending to important matters which had severely taxed her strength. Her shining dark skin looked ashen grey, her high forehead, surrounded by tangled woolly locks, was dripping with perspiration, and her thick lips were pale. Although she must have undergone great fatigue, she did not seem in need of rest; for, after greeting the ladies, apologizing for her long absence, and telling Barine that this time Dion had seemed to her half on the way to recovery, a rapid side glance at her mistress conveyed an entreaty that she would follow her into the next room.

But the language of the Nubian's eyes had not escaped the suspicious watchfulness of the anxious Barine and, overwhelmed with fresh terror, she begged that she might hear all.

Charmian ordered her maid to speak openly; but Anukis, ere she began, assured them that she had received the news she brought from a most trustworthy source—only it would make a heavy demand upon the resolution and courage of Barine, whom she had hoped to find in a very different mood. There was no time to lose. She was expected at the appointed place an hour after sunset.

Here Charmian interrupted the maid with the exclamation "Impossible!" and reminded her of the guards which Alexas, aided by Iras, who was thoroughly familiar with the palace, had stationed the day before in the anteroom, at all the doors— nay, even beneath the windows.

The Nubian replied that everything had been considered; but, to gain time, she must beg Barine to let her colour her skin and curl her hair while she was talking.

The surprise visible in the young beauty's face caused her to exclaim: "Only act with entire confidence. You shall learn everything directly.

There is so much to tell! On the way here I had planned how to relate the whole story in regular order, but it can't be done now. No, no! Whoever wants to save a flock of sheep from a burning shed must lead out the bell-wether first —the main thing, I mean—so I will begin with that, though it really comes last. The explanation of how all this——"

Here, like a cry of joy, Barine's exclamation interrupted her:

"I am to fly, and Dion knows it and will follow me! I see it in your face."

In fact, every feature of the dusky maid-servant's ugly face betrayed that pleasant thoughts were agitating her mind. Her black eyes flashed with fearless daring, and a smile beautified her big mouth and thick lips as she replied:

"A loving heart like yours understands the art of prophecy better than the chief priest of the great Serapis. Yes, my young mistress, he of whom you speak must disappear from this wicked city where so much evil threatens you both. He will certainly escape and, if the immortals aid us and we are wise and brave, you also. Whence the help comes can be told later. Now, the first thing is to transform you—don't be reluctant—into the ugliest woman in the world—black Anukis. You must escape from the palace in this disguise.—Now you know the whole plan, and while I get what is necessary from my chest of clothes, I beg you, mistress, to consider how we are to obtain the black stains for that ivory skin and golden hair."

With these words she left the room, but Barine flung herself into her friend's arms, exclaiming, amid tears and laughter: "Though I should be forced to remain forever as black and crooked as faithful Aisopion, if he did not withdraw his love, though I were obliged to go through fire and water—I would—— O Charmian! what changes so quickly as joy and sorrow? I would fain show some kindness to every one in the world, even to your Queen, who has brought all these troubles upon me."

The new-born hope had transformed the despairing woman into a happy one, and Charmian perceived it with grateful joy, secretly wishing that Cleopatra had listened to her appeal.

While examining the hair-dyes used by the Queen she saw, lurking in the background of what was still unexplained, and therefore confused her mind, fresh and serious perils. Barine, on the contrary, gazed across them to the anticipated meeting with her lover, and was full of the gayest expectation until the maid-servant's return.

The work of disfigurement began without delay. Anukis moved her lips as busily as her hands, and described in regular order all that had befallen her during the eventful day.

Barine listened with rising excitement, and her

joy increased as she beheld the path which had been smoothed for her by the care and wisdom of her friends. Charmian, on the contrary, became graver and more quiet the more distinctly she perceived the danger her favourite must encounter. Yet she could not help admitting that it would be a sin against Barine's safety, perhaps her very life, to withhold her from this well-considered plan of escape.

That it must be tried was certain; but as the moment which was to endanger the woman she loved drew nearer, and she could not help saying to herself that she was aiding an enterprise in opposition to the express command of the Queen and helping to execute a plan which threatened to rouse the indignation, perhaps the fury, of Cleopatra, a feeling of sorrow overpowered her. She feared nothing for herself. Not for a single instant did she think of the unpleasant consequences which Barine's escape might draw upon her. The burden on her soul was due only to the consciousness of having, for the first time, opposed the will of the sovereign, to fulfil whose desires and to promote whose aims had been the beloved duty of her life. Doubtless the thought crossed her mind that, by aiding Barine's escape, she was guarding Cleopatra from future repentance; probably she felt sure that it was her duty to help rescue this beautiful young life, whose bloom had been so cruelly assailed by tempest and hoar-frost, and which now had a prospect of the purest happiness; yet, though in itself commendable, the deed brought her into sharp conflict with the loftiest aims and aspirations of her life. And how much nearer than the other was the woman—she shrank from the word—whom she was about to betray, how much greater was Cleopatra's claim to her love and gratitude! Could she have any other emotion than thankfulness if the plan of escape succeeded? Yet she was reluctant to perform the task of making Barine's beautiful, symmetrical figure resemble the hunch-backed Nubian's, or to dip her fingers into the pomade intended for Cleopatra; and it grieved her to mar the beauty of Barine's luxuriant tresses by cutting off part of her thick fair braids.

True, these things could not be avoided, if the flight was to succeed, and the further Anukis advanced in her story, the fewer became her mistress's objections to the plan.

The conversation between Iras and Alexas, which had been overheard by the maid, already made it appear necessary to withdraw Barine and her lover from the power of such foes. The faithful man whom Anukis had found with Dion, whose name she did not mention and of whose home she said only that no safer hiding-place could be found, even by the mole which burrowed in the earth, really seemed to have been sent with Gorgias to Dion's couch by Fate itself. The control of the subterranean chambers in the Temple of Isis which had been bestowed on the architect, also appeared like a miracle.

Upon a small tablet, which the wise Aisopion had intentionally delayed handing to her mistress until now, were the lines:

"Archibius greets his sister Charmian. If I know your heart, it will be as hard for you as for me to share this plot, yet it must be done for the sake of her father, to save the life and happiness of his child. So it must fall to your lot to bring Barine to the Temple of Isis at the Corner of the Muses. She will find her lover there and, if possible, be wedded to him. As the sanctuary is so near, you need leave the palace only a short time. Do not tell Barine what we have planned. The disappointment would be too great if it should prove impracticable."

This letter and the arrangement it proposed transformed the serious scruples which shadowed Charmian's good-will into a joyous, nay, enthusiastic desire to render assistance. Barine's marriage to the man who possessed her heart was close at hand, and she was the daughter of Leonax, who had once been dear to her. Fear and doubt vanished as if scattered to the four winds, and when Aisopion's work of transformation was completed and Barine stood before her as the high-shouldered, dark-visaged, wrinkled maid, she could not help admitting that it would be easy to escape from the palace in that disguise.

She now told Barine that she intended to accompany her herself; and though the former's stained face forced her to refrain from kissing her friend, she plainly expressed to her and the faithful freedwoman the overflowing gratitude which filled her heart.

Anukis was left alone. After carefully removing all the traces of her occupation, as habit dictated, she raised her arms in prayer, beseeching the gods of her native land to protect the beautiful woman to whom she had loaned her own misshapen form, which had now been of genuine service, and who had gone forth to meet so many dangers, but also a happiness whose very hope had been denied to her.

Charmian had told her maid that if the Queen should inquire for her before Iras returned from the Choma to say that she had been obliged to leave the palace, and to supply her place. During their absence, when Charmian had been attacked by sickness, Cleopatra had often entrusted the care of her toilet to Aisopion, and had praised her skill.

The Queen's confidential attendant was followed as usual when she went out by a dark-skinned maid. Lanterns and lamps had already been lighted in the corridors of the spacious palace, and the court-yards were ablaze with torches and pitch-pans; but, brilliantly as they burned in many places, and numerous as were the guards, officers, eunuchs, clerks, soldiers, cooks, attendants, slaves, door-keepers, and messengers whom they passed, not one gave them more than a careless glance.

So they reached the last court-yard, and then came a moment when the hearts of both women seemed to stop beating—for the man whom they had most cause to dread, Alexas the Syrian, approached.

And he did not pass the fugitives, but stopped Charmian, and courteously, even obsequiously, informed her that he wished to get rid of the troublesome affair of her favourite, which had been assigned to him against his will, and therefore had determined to bring Barine to trial early the following morning.

The Syrian's body-servant attended his master, and while the former was talking with Charmian the latter turned to the supposed Nubian, tapped her lightly on the shoulder, and whispered: "Come this evening, as you did yesterday. You haven't finished the story of Prince Setnau."

The fugitive felt as if she had grown dumb and could never more regain the power of speech. Yet she managed to nod, and directly after the favourite bowed a farewell to Charmian. The Ligurian was obliged to follow his master, while Charmian and Barine passed through the gateway between the last pylons into the open air.

Here the sea-breeze seemed to waft her a joyous greeting from the realm of liberty and happiness, and the timid woman, amid all the perils which surrounded her, regained sufficient presence of mind to tell her friend what Alexas's slave had whispered—that Aisopion might remind him of it the same evening, and thus strengthen his belief that the Nubian had accompanied the Queen's confidante.

The way to the Temple of Isis was short. The stars showed that they would reach their destination in time; but a second delay unexpectedly occurred. From the steps leading to the cella of the sanctuary a procession, whose length seemed endless, came towards them. At the head of the train marched eight pastophori, bearing the image of Isis. Then came the basket-bearers of the goddess with several other priestesses, followed by the reader with an open book-roll. Behind him appeared the quaternary number of prophets, whose head, the chief priest, moved with stately dignity beneath a canopy. The rest of the priestly train bore in their hands manuscripts, sacred vessels, standards, and wreaths. The priestesses—some of whom, with garlands on their flowing hair, were already shaking the sistrum of Isis—mingled with the line of priests, their high voices blending with the deep notes of the men. Neokori, or temple servants, and a large number of worshippers of Isis, closed the procession, all wearing wreaths and carrying flowers. Torch and lantern bearers lighted the way, and the perfume of the incense rising from the little pan of charcoal in the hand of a bronze arm, which the pastophori waved to and fro, surrounded and floated after the procession.

The two women waiting for the train to pass saw it turn towards Lochias, and the conversation of the bystanders informed them that its object was to convey to "the new Isis," the Queen, the greeting of the goddess, and assure the sovereign of the divinity's remembrance of her in the hour of peril.

Cleopatra could not help accepting this friendly homage, and it was incumbent upon her to receive it wearing on her head the crown of Upper and Lower Egypt, and robed in all the ecclesiastical vestments which only her two most trusted attendants knew how to put on with the attention to details that custom required. This had never been entrusted to maids of inferior position like the Nubian; so Cleopatra would miss Charmian.

The thought filled her with fresh uneasiness and, when the steps were at last free, she asked herself anxiously how all this would end.

It seemed as if the fugitive and her companion had exposed themselves to this great peril in vain; for some of the temple servants were forcing back those who wished to enter the sanctuary, shouting that it would be closed until the return of the procession. Barine gazed timidly into Charmian's face; but, ere she could express her opinion, the tall figure of a man appeared on the temple steps. It was Archibius, who with grave composure bade them follow him, and silently led them around the sanctuary to a side door, through which, a short time before, a litter had passed, accompanied by several attendants.

Ascending a flight of steps within the long building, they reached the dimly lighted cella.

As in the Temple of Osiris at Abydos seven corridors, here three led to the same number of apartments, the holy place of the sanctuary. The central one was dedicated to Isis, that on the left to her husband Osiris, and that on the right to Horus, the son of the great goddess. Before it, scarcely visible in the dim light, stood the altars, loaded with sacrifices by Archibius.

Beside that of Horus was the litter which had been borne into the temple before the arrival of the women. From it, supported by two friends, descended a slender young man.

A hollow sound echoed through the pillared hall. The iron door at the main entrance of the temple had been closed. The shrill rattle that followed proceeded from the metal bolts which an old servant of the sanctuary had shot into the sockets.

Barine started, but neither inquired the cause of the noise nor perceived the wealth of objects here presented to the senses; for the man who, leaning on another's arm, approached the altar, was Dion, the lover who had perilled his life for her sake. Her eyes rested intently on his figure, her whole heart yearned towards him and, unable to control herself, she called his name aloud.

Charmian gazed anxiously around the group, but soon uttered a sigh of relief; for the tall man whose arm supported Dion was Gorgias, the worthy architect, his best friend, and the other, still taller and stronger, her own brother Archibius. Yonder figure, emerging from the disguise of wraps, was Berenike, Barine's mother. All trustworthy confidants! The only person whom she did not know was the handsome young man standing at her brother's side.

Barine, whose arm she still held, had struggled to escape to rush to her mother and lover; but Archibius had approached, and in a whisper warned her to be patient and to refrain from any greeting or question, "supposing," he added, " that you are willing to be married at this altar to Dion, the son of Eumenes."

Charmian felt Barine's arm tremble in hers at this suggestion, but the young beauty obeyed her friend's directions. She did not know what had befallen her, or whether, in the excess of happiness which overwhelmed her, to shout aloud in her exultant joy, or melt into silent tears of gratitude and emotion.

No one spoke. Archibius took a roll of manuscript from Dion's hand, presented himself before the assembled company as the bride's kyrios, or guardian, and asked Barine whether she so recognized him. Then he returned to Dion the marriage contract, whose contents he knew and approved, and informed those present that, in the marriage about to be solemnized, they must consider him the paranymphos, or best man, and Berenike as the bridesmaid, and they instantly lighted a torch at the fires burning on one of the altars. Archibius, as kyrios, joined the lovers' hands in the Egyptian—Barine's mother, as bridesmaid, in the Greek—manner, and Dion gave his bride a plain iron ring. It was the same one which his father had bestowed at his own wedding, and he whispered: "My mother valued it; now it is your turn to honour the ancient treasure."

After stating that the necessary sacrifices had been offered to Isis and Serapis, Zeus, Hera, and Artemis, and that the marriage between Dion, son of Eumenes, and Barine, daughter of Leonax, was concluded, Archibius shook hands with both.

Haste seemed necessary, for he permitted Berenike and his sister only time for a brief embrace, and Gorgias to clasp her hand and Dion's. Then he beckoned, and the newly made bride's mother followed him in tears, Charmian bewildered and almost stupefied. She did not fully realize the meaning of the event she had just witnessed until an old neokori had guided her and the others into the open air.

Barine felt as if every moment might rouse

her from a blissful dream, and yet she gladly told herself that she was awake, for the man walking before her, leaning on the arm of a friend, was Dion. True, she saw, even in the faint light of the dim temple corridor, that he was suffering. Walking appeared to be so difficult that she rejoiced when, yielding to Gorgias's entreaties, he entered the litter.

But where were the bearers?

She was soon to learn; for, even while she looked for them, the architect and the youth, in whom she had long since recognized Philotas, her grandfather's assistant, seized the poles.

"Follow us," said Gorgias, under his breath, and she obeyed, keeping close behind the litter, which was borne first down a broad and then a narrow staircase, and finally along a passage. Here a door stopped the fugitives; but the architect opened it and helped his friend out of the litter, which before proceeding farther he placed in a room filled with various articles discovered during his investigation of the subterranean temple chambers.

Hitherto not a word had been spoken. Now Gorgias called to Barine: "This passage is low— you must stoop. Cover your head, and don't be afraid if you meet bats. They have long been undisturbed. We might have taken you from the temple to the sea, and waited there, but it would probably have attracted attention and been dangerous. Courage, young wife of Dion! The corridor is long, and walking through it is difficult; but compared with the road to the mines, it is as smooth and easy as the Street of the King. If you think of your destination, the bats will seem like the swallows which announce the approach of spring."

Barine nodded gratefully to him; but she kissed the hand of Dion, who was moving forward painfully, leaning on the arm of his friend. The light of the torch carried by Gorgias's faithful foreman, who led the way, had fallen on her blackened arm, and when the little party advanced she kept behind the others. She thought it might be unpleasant for her lover to see her thus disfigured, and spared him, though she would gladly have remained nearer. As soon as the passage grew lower, the wounded man's friends took him in their arms, and their task was a hard one, for they were not only obliged to move onward bending low under the heavy burden, but also to beat off the bats which, frightened by the foreman's torch, flew up in hosts.

Barine's hair was covered, it is true, but at any other time the hideous creatures, which often brushed against her head and arms, would have filled her with horror and loathing. Now she scarcely heeded them; her eyes were fixed on the recumbent figure in the bearers' arms, the man to whom she belonged, body and soul, and whose patient suffering pierced her inmost heart. His head rested on the breast of Gorgias, who walked directly in front of her; the architect's stooping posture concealed his face, but his feet were visible and, whenever they twitched, she fancied he was in pain. Then she longed to press forward to his side, wipe the perspiration from his brow in the hot, low corridor, and whisper words of love and encouragement.

This she was sometimes permitted to do when the friends put down their heavy burden. True, they allowed themselves only brief intervals of rest, but they were long enough to show her how the sufferer's strength was failing. When they at last reached their destination, Philotas was forced to exert all his strength to support the exhausted man, while Gorgias cautiously opened the door. It led to a flight of sea-washed steps close to the garden of Didymus, which as a child she had often used with her brother to float a little boat upon the water.

The architect opened the door only a short distance; he was expected, for Barine soon heard him whisper, and suddenly the door was flung wide. A tall man raised Dion and bore him into the open air. While she was still gazing after him, a second figure of equal size approached her and, hastily begging her permission, lifted her in his arms like a child, and as she inhaled the cool night air and felt the water through which her bearer waded splash up and wet her feet, her eyes sought her new-made husband—but in vain; the night was very dark, and the lights on the shore did not reach this spot so far below the walls of the quay.

Barine was frightened; but a few minutes after the outlines of a large fishing boat loomed through the darkness, dimly illumined by the harbour lights, and the next instant the giant who carried her placed her on the deck, and a deep voice whispered: "All's well. I'll bring some wine at once."

Then Barine saw her husband lying motionless on a couch which had been prepared for him in the prow of the boat. Bending over him, she perceived that he had fainted, and while rubbing his forehead with the wine, raising his head on her lap, cheering him, and afterwards by the light of a small lantern carefully renewing the bandage on his shoulder, she did not notice that the vessel was moving through the water until the boatman set the triangular sail.

She had not been told where the boat was bearing her, and she did not ask. Any spot that she could share with Dion was welcome. The more lonely the place, the more she could be to him. How her heart swelled with gratitude and love! When she bent over him, kissed his forehead, and felt how feverishly it burned, she thought, "I will nurse you back to health," and raised her eyes and soul to her favourite god, to whom she owed the gift of song, and who understood everything beautiful and pure, to thank

Phœbus Apollo and beseech him to pour his rays the next morning on a convalescent man. While she was still engaged in prayer the boat touched the shore. Again strong arms bore her and Dion to the land, and when her foot touched the solid earth, her rescuer, the freedman Pyrrhus, broke the silence, saying: "Welcome, wife of Dion, to our island! True, you must be satisfied to take us as we are. But if you are as content with us as we are glad to serve you and your lord, who is ours also, the hour of leave-taking will be far distant."

Then, leading the way to the house, he showed her as her future apartments two large whitewashed rooms, whose sole ornament was their exquisite neatness.

On the threshold stood Pyrrhus's grey-haired wife, a young woman, and a girl scarcely beyond childhood; but the older one modestly welcomed Barine, and also begged her to accept their hospitality. Recovery was rapid in the pure air of the Serpent Isle. She herself, and—she pointed to the others—her oldest son's wife, and her own daughter, Dione, would be ready to render her any service.

CHAPTER XVI.

Brothers and sisters are rarely talkative when they are together. As Charmian went to Lochias with Archibius, it was difficult for her to find words, the events of the past few hours had agitated her so deeply. Archibius, too, could not succeed in turning his thoughts in any other direction, though important and far more momentous things claimed his attention.

They walked on silently side by side. In reply to his sister's inquiry where the newly wedded pair were to be concealed, he had answered that, spite of her trustworthiness, this must remain a secret. To her second query, how had it been possible to use the interior of the Temple of Isis without interruption, he also made a guarded reply.

In fact, it was the control of the subterranean corridors of the sanctuary which had suggested to Gorgias the idea of carrying Dion through them to Pyrrhus's fishing-boat. To accomplish this it was only necessary to have the Temple of Isis, which usually remained open day and night, left to the fugitive's friends for a short time; and this was successfully managed.

The historian Timagenes, who had come from Rome as ambassador and claimed the hospitality of his former pupil Archibius, had been empowered to offer Cleopatra recognition of her own and her children's right to the throne, and a full pardon, if she would deliver Mark Antony into the hands of Octavianus, or have him put to death.

The Alexandrian Timagenes considered this demand both just and desirable, because it promised to deliver his native city from the man whose despotic arrogance menaced its freedom, and whose lavish generosity and boundless love of splendour diminished its wealth. To Rome, as whose representative the historian appeared, this man's mere existence meant constant turmoil and civil war. At the restoration of the flute-player by Gabinius and Mark Antony, Timagenes had been carried into slavery. Later, when, after his freedom had been purchased by the son of Sulla, he succeeded in attaining great influence in Rome, he still remained hostile to Mark Antony, and it had been a welcome charge to work against him in Alexandria. He hoped to find an ally in Archibius, whose loyal devotion to the Queen he knew. Arius, Barine's uncle and Octavianus's former tutor, would also aid him. The most powerful support of his mission, however, could be rendered by the venerable chief priest, the head of the whole Egyptian hierarchy. He had shown the latter that Antony, in any case, was a lost man, and Egypt was in the act of dropping like a ripe fruit into the lap of Octavianus. It would soon be in his power to give the country whatever degree of liberty and independence he might choose. The Cæsar had the sole disposal of the Queen's fate also, and whoever desired to see her remain on the throne must strive to gain the good-will of Octavianus.

The wise Anubis had considered all these things, but he owed to Timagenes the hint that Arius was the man whom Octavianus most trusted. So the august prelate secretly entered into communication with Barine's uncle. But the dignity of his high office, and the feebleness of extreme age, forbade Anubis to seek the man who was suspected of friendship for the Romans. He had therefore sent his trusted secretary, the young Serapion, to make a compact as his representative with the friend of Octavianus, whose severe injuries prevented his leaving the house to go to the chief priest.

During Timagenes's negotiations with the secretary and Arius, Archibius came to entreat Barine's uncle to do everything in his power to save his niece; and, as all the Queen's friends were anxious to prevent an act which, in these times of excitement, could not fail, on account of its connection with Dion, a member of the Council, to rouse a large number of the citizens against her, Serapion, as soon as he was made aware of the matter, eagerly protested his readiness to do his best to save the imperilled lovers. He cared nothing for Barine or Dion as individuals, but he doubtless would have been ready to make a still greater sacrifice to win the influential Archibius, and especially Arius, who would have great power through Octavianus, the rising sun.

The men had just begun to discuss plans for saving Barine, when the Nubian appeared and told Archibius what had been arranged beside Dion's sick-bed by the freedman and Gorgias. The escape of the fugitives depended solely upon their reaching the boat unseen, and the surest way to accomplish this was to use the subterranean passage which the architect had again opened.

Archibius, to whom the representative of the chief priest had offered his aid, now took the others into his confidence, and Arius proposed that Barine should marry Dion in the Temple of Isis, and the couple should afterwards be guided through the secret passage to the boat. This proposal was approved, and Serapion promised to reserve the sanctuary for the wedding of the fugitives for a short time after the departure of the procession, which was to take place at sunset. In return for this service another might perhaps soon be requested from the friend of Octavianus, who greeted his promise with grateful warmth.

"The priesthood," said Serapion, "takes sides with all who are unjustly persecuted, and in this case bestows aid the more willingly on account of its great anxiety to guard the Queen from an act which would be difficult to approve." As for the fugitives, so far as he could see, only two possibilities were open to them: Cleopatra would cleave to Mark Antony and go—would that the immortals might avert it!—to ruin, or she would sacrifice him and save her throne and life. In both cases the endangered lovers could soon return uninjured—the Queen had a merciful heart, and never retained anger long if no guilt existed.

The details of the plan were then settled by Archibius, Anukis, and Berenike, who was with the family of Arius, and the decision was communicated to the architect. Archibius had maintained the same silence concerning the destination of the fugitives towards the men composing the council and Barine's mother as to his sister. With regard to the mission of Timagenes and the political questions which occupied his mind, he gave Charmian only the degree of information necessary to explain the plan she so lovingly promoted; but she had no desire to know more. On the way home her mind was wholly absorbed by the fear that Cleopatra had missed her services and discovered Barine's flight. True, she mentioned the Queen's desire to place her children in Archibius's charge, but she could not give him full particulars until she reached her own apartments.

Her absence had not been noticed. The Regent Mardion had received the procession in the

Queen's name, for Cleopatra had driven into the city, no one knew where.

Charmian entered her apartments with a lighter heart. Anukis opened the door to them. She had remained undisturbed, and it was a pleasure to Archibius to give the faithful, clever freedwoman an account of the matter with his own lips. He could have bestowed no richer reward upon the modest servant, who listened to his words as if they were a revelation. When she disclaimed the thanks with which he concluded, protesting that she was the person under obligation, the expression was sincere. Her keen intellect instantly recognized the aristocrat's manner of addressing an equal or an inferior; and he who, in her eyes, was the first of men, had described the course of events as though she had stood on the same level. The Queen herself might have been satisfied with the report.

When she left Charmian's rooms to join the other servants, she told herself that she was an especially favoured mortal; and when a young cook teased her about her head being sunk between her shoulders, she answered, laughing: "My shoulders have grown so high because I shrug them so often at the fools who jeer at me and yet are not half so happy and grateful."

Charmian, sorely wearied, had flung herself into an arm-chair, and Archibius took his place opposite to her. They were happy in each other's society, even when silent; but to-day the hearts of both were so full that they fared like those who are so worn out by fatigue that they cannot sleep. How much they had to tell each other!—yet it was long ere Charmian broke the silence and returned to the subject of the Queen's wish, describing to her brother Cleopatra's visit to the house which the children had built, how kind and cordial she had been; yet, a few minutes later, incensed by the mere mention of Barine's name, she had dismissed her so ungraciously.

"I do not know what you intend," she said in conclusion, "but, notwithstanding my love for her, I must perhaps decide in favour of what is most difficult, for—when she learns that it was I who withdrew the daughter of Leonax from her and the base Alexas—what treatment can I expect, especially as Iras no longer gives me the same affection, and shows that she has forgotten my love and care? This will increase, and the worst of the matter is, that if the Queen begins to favour her, I cannot justly reproach her, for Iras is keener-witted, and has a more active brain. Statecraft was always odious to me. Iras, on the contrary, is delighted with the opportunity to speak on subjects connected with the government of the country, and especially the ceaseless, momentous game with Rome and the men who guide her destiny."

" That game is lost," Archibius broke in with

so much earnestness that Charmian started, repeating in a low, timid tone:

"Lost?"

"Forever," said Archibius, "unless——"

"The Olympians be praised—that there is still a doubt."

"Unless Cleopatra can decide to commit an act which will force her to be faithless to herself, and destroy her noble image through all future generations."

"How?"

"Whenever you learn it, will be too soon."

"And suppose she should do it, Archibius? You are her most trusted confidant. She will place in your charge what she loves more than she does herself."

"More? You mean, I suppose, the children?"

"The children! Yes, a hundred times yes. She loves them better than aught else on earth. For them, believe me, she would be ready to go to her death."

"Let us hope so."

"And you—were she to commit the horrible deed—I can only suspect what it is. But should she descend from the height which she has hitherto occupied—would you still be ready——"

"With me," he interrupted quietly, "what she does or does not do matters nothing. She is unhappy and will be plunged deeper and deeper into misery. I know this, and it constrains me to exert my utmost powers in her service. I am hers as the hermit consecrated to Serapis belongs to the god. His every thought must be devoted to him. To the deity who created him he dedicates body and soul until the death to which he dooms him. The bonds which unite me to this woman—you know their origin—are not less indestructible. Whatever she desires whose fulfilment will not force me to despise myself is granted in advance."

"She will never require such things from the friend of her childhood," cried Charmian. Then, approaching him with both arms extended joyfully, she exclaimed: "Thus you ought to speak and feel, and therein is the answer to the question which has agitated my soul since yesterday. Barine's flight, the favour and disfavour of Cleopatra, Iras, my poor head, which abhors politics, while at this time the Queen needs keen-sighted confidants——"

"By no means," her brother interrupted. "It is for men alone to give counsel in these matters. Accursed be women's gossip over their toilet tables! It has already scattered to the four winds many a well-considered plan of the wisest heads, and an Iras could never be more fatal to statecraft than just at the present moment, had not Fate already uttered the final verdict."

"Then hence with these scruples," cried Charmian eagerly; "my doubts are at an end! As usual, you point out the right path. I had thought of returning to the country estate we call Irenia—the abode of peace—or to our beloved little palace at Kanopus, to spend the years which may still be allotted to me, and return to everything that made my childhood beautiful. The philosophers, the flowers in the garden, the poets—even the new Roman ones, of whose works Timagenes sent us such charming specimens—would enliven the solitude. The child, the daughter of the man whose love I renounced, and afterwards perhaps her sons and daughters, would fill the place of my own. As they would have been dear to Leonax, I, too, would have loved them! This is the guise in which the future has appeared to me in many a quiet hour. But shall Charmian—who, when her heart throbbed still more warmly and life lay fair before her, laid her first love upon the altar of sacrifice for her royal playfellow—abandon Cleopatra in misfortune from mere selfish scruples? No, no!—Like you, I too belong—come what may—to the Queen."

She gazed into her brother's face, sure of his approval but, waving his uplifted hand, he answered gravely: "No, Charmian! What I, a man, can assume, might be fatal to you, a woman. The present is not sweet enough for me to embitter it with wormwood from the future. And yet—— You must cast one glance into its gloomy domain, in order to understand me. You can be silent, and what you now learn will be a secret between us. Only one thing"—here he lowered the loud tones of his deep voice—"only one thing can save her: the murder of Antony, or an act of shameless treachery which would deliver him into Octavianus's power. This is the proposal Timagenes brought."

"This?" she asked in a hollow tone, her grey head drooping.

"This," he repeated firmly. "And if she succumbs to the temptation, she will be faithless to the love which has coursed through her whole life as the Nile flows through the land of her ancestors. Then, Charmian, stay, stay under any circumstances, cling to her more firmly than ever, for then, then, my sister, she will be more wretched—ten, a hundred fold more wretched than if Octavianus deprives her of everything, perhaps even life itself."

"Nor will I leave her, come what may. I will remain at her side until the end," cried Charmian eagerly. But Archibius, without noticing the enthusiastic ardor, so unusual to his sister's quiet nature, calmly continued: "She won your heart also, and it seems impossible for you to desert her. Many have shared our feelings; and it is no disgrace to any one. Misfortune is a weapon which cleaves base natures like a sword, yet like a hammer welds noble ones more closely. To you, therefore, it now seems doubly difficult to leave her, but you need love. The right to live and guard yourself from the most pitiable retrogression is your due, as much as that of the rare woman on the throne. So long as you are sure of her love, remain with her, and show your devotion in every situation until the end. But the motives which were drawing you away to books, flowers, and children, weigh heavily in the balance, and if you lack the anchor of her favour and love, I shall see you perish miserably. The frost emanating from Cleopatra, if her heart grew cold to you, the pin-pricks with which Iras would assail you, were you defenceless, would kill you. This must not be, sister; we will guard against it—— Do not interrupt me. The counsel I advise you to follow has been duly weighed. If you see that the Queen still loves you as in former days, cling to her; but should you learn the contrary, bid her farewell to-morrow. My Irenia is yours——"

"But she *does* love me, and even should she no longer——"

"The test is at hand. We will leave the decision to her. You shall confess that you were the culprit who aided Barine to escape her power to punish."

"Archibius!"

"If you did not, a series of falsehoods must ensue. Try whether the petty qualities in her nature, which urged her to commit the fate of Leonax's daughter to unworthy hands, are more powerful than the nobler ones. Try whether she is worthy of the self-sacrificing fidelity which you have given her all your life. If she remains the same as before, spite of this admission——"

Here he was interrupted by Anukis, who asked if her mistress would see Iras at this late hour.

"Admit her," replied Archibius, after hastily exchanging glances with his sister, whose face had paled at his demand. He perceived it and, as the servant withdrew, he clasped her hand, saying with earnest affection: "I gave you my opinion, but at our age we must take counsel with ourselves, and you will find the right path."

"I have already found it," she answered softly with downcast eyes. "This visitor brought a speedy decision. I must not feel ashamed in Iras's presence."

She had scarcely finished speaking when the Queen's younger confidante entered. She was excited and, after casting a searching glance around the familiar room, she asked, after a curt greeting: "No one knows where the Queen has gone. Mardion received the procession in her place. Did she take you into her confidence?"

Charmian answered in the negative, and inquired whether Antony had arrived, and how she had found him.

"In a pitiable state," was the reply. "I hastened hither to prevent the Queen from visiting him, if possible. She would have received a rebuff. It is horrible."

"The disappointment of Paraetonium is added to the other burdens," observed Archibius.

"A feather compared with the rest," cried Iras

indignantly. "What a spectacle! A shrivelled soul, never too large, in the body of a powerful giant. Disaster crushes the courage of the descendant of Herakles. The weakling will drag the Queen's splendid courage with him into the dust."

"We will do our best to prevent it," replied Archibius firmly. "The immortals have placed you and Charmian at her side to sustain her, if her own strength fails. The time to test your powers has arrived."

"I know my duty," replied Iras austerely.

"Prove it!" said Archibius earnestly. "You think you have cause for anger against Charmian."

"Whoever treats my foes so tenderly can doubtless dispense with my affection. Where is your ward?"

"That you shall learn later," replied Charmian advancing. "But when you do know, you will have still better reason to doubt my love; yet it was only to save one dear to me from misery, certainly not to grieve you, that I stepped between you and Barine. And now let me say—had you wounded me to the quick, and everything dear to the Greek heart called to me for vengeance—I should impose upon myself whatever constraint might be necessary to deny the impulse, because this breast contains a love stronger, more powerful, than the fiercest hate. And this love we both share. Hate me, strive to wound and injure one at whose side you have hitherto stood like a daughter, but beware of robbing me of the strength and freedom which I need, to be and to offer to my royal mistress all the assistance in my power. I have just been consulting my brother about leaving Cleopatra's service."

" Now?" Iras broke in vehemently. " No, no! Not that! It must not be! She cannot spare you now."

" More easily, perhaps, than you," replied Charmian; " yet in many things my services might be hard to replace."

" Nothing under the sun *could* do it," cried Iras eagerly. " If, in these days of trouble, she should lose you too——"

" Still darker ones are approaching," interrupted Archibius positively. " Perhaps you will learn all to-morrow. Whether Charmian yields to her desire for rest, or continues in the service of the Queen, depends on you. If you wish her to remain you must not render it too hard for her to do so. We three, my child, are perhaps the only persons at this court to whom the Queen's happiness is more than their own, and therefore we should permit no incident, whatever name it may bear, to cloud our harmony."

Iras threw back her head with angry pride, exclaiming passionately: " Was it I who injured you? I do not know in what respect. But you and Charmian—though you have so long been aware that this heart was closed against every love save one—stepped between me and the man for whom I have yearned since childhood, and built the bridge which united Dion and Barine. I held the woman I hated in my grasp, and thanked the immortals for the boon; but you two—it is not difficult to guess the secret you are still trying to keep from me—you aided her to escape. You have robbed me of my revenge; you have again placed the singer in the path where she must find the man to whom I have a better and older claim, and who perhaps may still be considering which of us two will be the better mistress of his house, if Alexas and his worthy brother do not arrange matters so that we must both content ourselves with thinking tenderly of a dead man. That is why I believe that I am no longer indebted to you, that Charmian has more than repaid herself for all the kindness she has ever showed me."

With these words she hurried to the door, but paused on the threshold, exclaiming: "This is the state of affairs; yet I am ready to serve the Queen hand in hand with you as before; for you two—as I have said—are necessary to her. In other respects—I shall follow my own path."

CHAPTER XVII.

CLEOPATRA had sought the venerable Anubis, who now, as the priest of Alexander, at the age of eighty, ruled the whole hierarchy of the country. It was difficult for him to leave his arm-chair, but he had been carried to the observatory to examine the adverse result of the observation made by the Queen herself. The position of the stars, however, had been so unfavourable that the more deeply Cleopatra entered into these matters, the less easy he found it to urge the mitigating influences of distant planets, which he had at first pointed out.

In his reception-hall, however, the chief priest had assured her that the independence of Egypt and the safety of her own person lay in her hands; only—the planets showed this—a terrible sacrifice was required—a sacrifice of which his dignity, his eighty years, and his love for her alike forbade him to speak. Cleopatra was accustomed to hear these mysterious sayings from his lips, and interpreted them in her own way. Many motives had induced her to seek the venerable prelate at this late hour. In difficult situations he had often aided her with good counsel; but this time she was not led to him by the magic cup of Nektanebus, which the eight pastophori who accompanied it had that day restored to the temple, for since the battle of Actium the superb vessel had been a source of constant anxiety to her.

Cleopatra had now asked the teacher of her childhood the direct question whether the cup—a wide, shallow vessel, with a flat, polished bottom—could really have induced Antony to leave the battle and follow her ere the victory was decided. She had used it just before the conflict between the galleys, and this circumstance led Anubis to answer positively in the affirmative.

Long ago the marvellous chalice had been exhibited to her among the temple treasures, and she was told that every one who induced another person to be reflected from its shining surface obtained the mastery over his will. Her wish to possess it, however, was not gratified, and she did not ask for it again until the limitless devotion and ardent love of Antony had seemed less fervent than of yore. From that time she had never ceased to urge her aged friend to place the wondrous cup in her keeping. At first he had absolutely refused, predicting that its use would bring misfortune upon her; but when her request was followed by an imperative command, and the goblet was entrusted to her, Anubis himself believed that this *one* vessel did possess the magic power attributed to it. He deemed that the drinking-cup afforded the strongest proof of the magic art, far transcending human ability, of the great goddess by whose aid King Nektanebus—who, according to tradition, was the father of Alexander the Great—was said to have made the vessel in the Isis island of Philæ.

Anubis had intended to remind Cleopatra of his refusal, and show her the great danger incurred by mortals who strove to use powers beyond their sphere. It had been his purpose to bid her remember Phaeton, who had almost kindled a conflagration in the world when he attempted, in the chariot of his father, Phœbus Apollo, to guide the horses of the sun. But this was unnecessary, for he had scarcely assented to the question ere, with passionate vehemence, she ordered him to destroy before her eyes the cup which had brought so much misfortune.

The priest feigned that her desire harmonized with a resolution which he had himself formed.

In fact, before her arrival, he had feared that the goblet might be used in some fatal manner if Octavianus should take possession of the city and country, and the wonder-working vessel should fall into his hands. Nektanebus had made the cup for Egypt. To wrest it from the foreign ruler was acting in the spirit of the last king in whose veins had flowed the blood of the Pharaohs, and who had toiled with enthusiastic devotion for the independence and liberty of his people. To destroy this man's marvellous work rather than deliver it to the Roman conqueror seemed to the chief priest, after the Queen's command, a sacred duty, and as such he represented it to be when he commanded the smelting furnace to be fired and the cup transformed into a shapeless mass before the eyes of Cleopatra.

While the metal was melting he eagerly told the Queen how easily she could dispense with the vessel which owed its magic power to the mighty Isis.

The spell of woman's charms was also a gift of the goddess. It would suffice to render Antony's heart soft and yielding as the fire melted the gold. Perhaps the Imperator had forfeited, with the Queen's respect, her love—the most priceless of blessings. He, Anubis, would regard this as a great boon of the Deity; "for," he concluded, "Mark Antony is the cliff which will shatter every effort to secure to my royal mistress undiminished the heritage which has come to her and her children from their ancestors, and preserve the independence and prosperity of this beloved land. This cup was a costly treasure. The throne and prosperity of Egypt are worthy of greater sacrifices. But I know that there is none harder for a woman to make than her love."

The meaning of the old man's words Cleopatra

learned the following morning, when she granted the first interview to Timagenes, Octavianus's envoy.

The keen-witted, brilliant man, who had been one of her best teachers and with whom, when a pupil, she had had many an argument, was kindly received, and fulfilled his commission with consummate skill.

The Queen listened attentively to his representations, showed him that her own intellect had not lost in flexibility, though it had gained power; and when she dismissed him, with rich gifts and gracious words, she knew that she could preserve the independence of her beloved native land and retain the throne for herself and her children if she would surrender Antony to the conqueror or to him, as "the person acting," or—these were Timagenes's own words—"remove him forever from the play whose end she had the power to render either brilliant or fateful."

When she was again alone her heart throbbed so passionately and her soul was in such a tumult of agitation that she felt unable to attend the appointed meeting of the Council of the crown. She deferred the session until the following day, and resolved to go out upon the sea, to endeavour to regain her composure.

Antony had refused to see her. This wounded her. The thought of the goblet and its evil influences had by no means passed from her memory with the destruction of the vessel caused by one of those outbursts of passion to which, in these days of disaster, she yielded more frequently than usual. On the contrary, she felt the necessity of being alone, to collect her thoughts and strive to dispel the clouds from her troubled soul.

The beaker had been one of the treasures of Isis, and the memory of it recalled hours during which, in former days, she had often found composure in the temple of the goddess. She wished to seek the sanctuary unnoticed and, accompanied only by Iras and the chief Introducer,* went, closely veiled, to the neighbouring temple at the Corner of the Muses.

But she failed to find the object of her pilgrimage. The throng which filled it to pray and offer sacrifices, and the fear of being recognized, destroyed her calmness.

She was in the act of retiring, when Gorgias, the architect, followed by an assistant carrying surveying instruments, advanced towards her. She instantly called him to her side, and he informed her how wonderfully Fate itself seemed to favour her plan of building. The mob had destroyed the house of the old philosopher Didymus, and the grey-haired sage, to whom he had offered the shelter of his home, was now ready to transfer the property inherited from his ancestors, if her Majes-

---

* Marshal of the court.

ty would assure him and his family of her protection.

Then she asked to see the architect's plan for joining the museum to the sanctuary, and became absorbed in the first sketch, to which he had devoted part of the night and morning. He showed it, and with eager urgency Cleopatra commanded him to begin the building as soon as possible and pursue the work night and day. What usually required months must be completed in weeks.

Iras and the "Introducer," clad in plain garments, had waited for her in the temple court and, joined by the architect, accompanied her to the unpretending litter standing at one of the side gates but, instead of entering it, she ordered Gorgias to attend her to the garden.

The inspection proved that the architect was right and, even if the mausoleum occupied a portion of it, and the street which separated it from the Temple of Isis were continued along the shore of the sea, the remainder would still be twice as large as the one belonging to the palace at Lochias.

Cleopatra's thorough examination showed Gorgias that she had some definite purpose in view. Her inquiry whether it would be possible to connect it with the promontory of Lochias indicated what she had in mind, and the architect answered in the affirmative. It was only necessary to tear down some small buildings belonging to the Crown and a little temple of Berenike at the southern part of the royal harbour. The arm of the Agathodæmon Canal which entered here had been bridged long ago.

The new scene which would result from this change had been conjured before the Queen's mental vision with marvellous celerity, and she described it in brief, vivid language to the architect. The garden should remain, but must be enlarged from the Lochias to the bridge. Thence a covered colonnade would lead to the palace. After Gorgias had assured her that all this could easily be arranged, she gazed thoughtfully at the ground for a time, and then gave orders that the work should be commenced at once, and requested him to spare neither means nor men.

Gorgias foresaw a period of feverish toil, but it did not daunt him. With such a master builder he was ready to roof the whole city. Besides, the commission delighted him because it proved that the woman whose mausoleum was to rise from the earth so swiftly still thought of enhancing the pleasures of existence; for, though she wished the garden to remain unchanged, she desired to see the colonnade and the remainder of the work constructed of costly materials and in beautiful forms. When she bade him farewell, Gorgias kissed her robe with ardent enthusiasm.

What a woman! True, she had not even raised her veil, and was attired in plain dark clothing, but every gesture revealed the most perfect grace.

The arm and hand with which she pointed now here, now there, again seemed to him fairly instinct with life; and he, who deemed perfection of form of so much value, found it difficult to avert his eyes from her marvellous symmetry. And her whole figure! What lines, what genuine aristocratic elegance, and warm, throbbing life!

That morning when Helena, now an inmate of his own home, greeted him, he had essayed to compare her, mentally, with Cleopatra, but speedily desisted. The man to whom Hebe proffers nectar does not ask for even the best wine of Byblus. A feeling of grateful, cheerful satisfaction, difficult to describe, stole over him when the reserved, quiet Helena addressed him so warmly and cordially; but the image of Cleopatra constantly thrust itself between them, and it was difficult for him to understand himself. He had loved many women in succession, and now his heart throbbed for two at once, and the Queen was the brighter of the two stars whose light entranced him. Therefore his honest soul would have considered it a crime to woo Helena now.

Cleopatra knew what an ardent admirer she had won in the able architect, and the knowledge pleased her. She had used no goblet to gain *him*. Doubtless he would begin to build the mausoleum the next morning. The vault must have space for several coffins. Antony had more than once expressed the desire to be buried beside her, wherever he might die, and this had occurred ere she possessed the beaker. She must in any case grant him the same favour, no matter in what place or by whose hand he met death, and the bedimmed light of his existence was but too evidently nearing extinction. If she spared him, Octavianus would strike him from the ranks of the living, and she—— Again she was overpowered by the terrible, feverish restlessness which had induced her to command the destruction of the goblet, and had brought her to the temple. She could not return in this mood to meet her councillors, receive visitors, greet her children. This was the birthday of the twins; Charmian had reminded her of it and undertaken to provide the gifts. How could she have found time and thought for such affairs?

She had returned from the chief priest late in the evening, yet had asked for a minute description of the condition in which they found Mark Antony. The report made by Iras harmonized with the state in which she had herself seen him during and after the battle. Ay, his brooding gloom seemed to have deepened. Charmian had helped her dress in the morning, and had been on the point of making her difficult confession, and owning that she had aided Barine to escape the punishment of her royal mistress; but ere she could begin, Timagenes was announced, for Cleopatra had not risen from her couch until a late hour.

The object for which the Queen had sought the temple had not been gained; but the consultation with Gorgias had diverted her mind, and the emotions which the thought of her last resting-place had evoked now drowned everything else, as the roar of the surf dominates the twittering of the swallows on the rocky shore.

Ay, she needed calmness! She must weigh and ponder over many things in absolute quietude, and this she could not obtain at Lochias. Then her glance rested upon the little sanctuary of Berenike, which she had ordered removed to make room for a garden near at hand, where the children could indulge their love of creative work. It was empty. She need fear no interruption there. The interior contained only a single, quiet, pleasant chamber, with the image of Berenike. The "Introducer" commanded the guard to admit no other visitors, and soon the little white marble, circular room with its vaulted roof received the Queen. She sank down on one of the bronze benches opposite to the statue. All was still; in this cool silence her mind, trained to thought, could find that for which it longed—clearness of vision, a plain understanding of her own feelings and position in the presence of the impending decision.

At first her thoughts wandered to and fro like a dove ere it chooses the direction of its flight; but after the question why she was having a tomb built so hurriedly, when she would be permitted to live, her mind found the right track. Among the Scythian guards, the Mauritanians, and Blemmyes in the army there were plenty of savage fellows whom a word from her lips and a handful of gold would have set upon the vanquished Antony, as the huntsman's "Seize him!" urges the hounds. A hint, and among the wretched magicians and Magians in the Rhakotis, the Egyptian quarter of the city, twenty men would have assassinated him by poison or wily snares; one command to the Macedonians in the guard of the Mellakes or youths, and he would be a captive that very day, and to-morrow, if she so ordered, on the way to Asia, whither Octavianus, as Timagenes told her, had gone.

What prevented her from grasping the gold, giving the hint, issuing the command?

Doubtless she thought of the magic goblet, now melted, which had constrained him to cast aside honour, fame, and power, as worthless rubbish, in order to obey her behest not to leave her; but though this remembrance burdened her soul, it had no decisive influence. It was no one thing which prisoned her hand and lips, but every fibre of her being, every pulsation of her heart, every glance back into the past to the confines of childhood.

Yet she listened to other thoughts also. They reminded her of her children, the elation of power, love for the land of her ancestors, and the peril which menaced it without her, the bliss of seeing the light, and the darkness, the silence, the dull rigidity of death, the destruction of the body and the mind cherished and developed with so much care and toil, the horrible torture which might be associated with the transition from life to death—the act of dying. And what lay before her in the existence which lasted an eternity? When she no longer breathed beneath the sun, even if the death hour was deferred, and she found that not Epicurus, who believed that with death all things ended, had been right, but the ancient teachings of the Egyptians, what would await her in that world beyond the grave if she purchased a few more years of life by the murder or betrayal of her lover, her husband?

Yet perhaps the punishments inflicted upon the condemned were but bugbears invented by the priesthood, which guarded the regulation of the state in order to curb the unruly conduct of the populace and terrify the turbulent transgressors of the law. And, whispered the daring Greek spirit, in the abode of the condemned, not in the Garden of Aalu, the Elysian Fields of the Egyptians, she would meet her father and mother and all her wicked ancestors down to Euergetes I, who was succeeded by the infamous Philopater. Thus the thought of the other world became an antecedent so uncertain as to permit no definite inference, and might therefore be left out of the account. How would—this must be the form of the question—the years purchased by the murder or betrayal of one whom she loved shape themselves for her?

During the night the image of the murdered man would drive sleep from her couch, and the Furies, the Diræ, as the Roman Antony called them, who pursue murderers with the serpent scourge, were no idle creations of poetic fancy, but fully symbolized the restlessness of the criminal, driven to and fro by the pangs of conscience. The chief good, the painless happiness of the Epicureans, was forever lost to those burdened by such guilt.

And during the hours of the day and evening? Ay, then she would be free to heap pleasure on pleasure. But for whom were the festivals to be celebrated; with whom could she share them? For many a long year no banquet, no entertainment had given her enjoyment without Mark Antony. For whom did she adorn herself or strive to stay the vanishing charm? And how soon would anguish of soul utterly destroy the spell, which was slowly, slowly, yet steadily diminishing, and, when the mirror revealed wrinkles which the skill of no Olympus could efface, when she—— No, she was not created to grow old! Did the few years of life which must contain so much misery really possess a value great enough to surrender the right of being called by present and future generations the bewitching Cleopatra, the most irresistible of women?

And the children?

Yes, it would have been delightful to see them grow up and occupy the throne, but serious, decisive doubts soon blended even with an idea so rich in joy.

How glorious to greet Cæsarion as sovereign of the world in Octavianus's place! But how could the dreamer, whose first love affair had caused the total sacrifice of dignity and violation of the law, and who now seemed to have once more relapsed into the old state of torpor, attain the position?

The other children inspired fair hopes, and how beautiful it appeared to the mother's heart to see Antonius Helios as King of Egypt; Cleopatra Selene with her first child in her arms; and little Alexander a noble statesman and hero, rich in virtue and talents! Yet, what would they, Antony's children, whose education she hoped Archibius would direct, feel for the mother who had been their father's murderess?

She shuddered at the thought, remembering the hours when her childish heart had shed tears of blood over the infamous mother whom her father had execrated. And Queen Tryphœna, whom history recorded as a monster, had not killed her husband, but merely thrust him from the throne.

Arsinoe's execrations of her mother and sister came back to her memory, and the thought that the rosy lips of the twins and her darling Alexander could ever open to curse her, the idea that the children would ever raise their beloved hands to point at her, the wicked murderess of their father, with horror and scorn—— No, no, and again no! She would not purchase a few more years of valueless life at the cost of this humiliation and shame.

Purchase of whom?

Of that Octavianus who had robbed her son of the heritage of his father, Cæsar, and whose mention in the will was like an imputation on her fidelity—the cold-hearted, calculating upstart, whose nature from their first meeting in Rome had repelled, rebuffed, chilled her; of the man by whose cajolery and power her husband—for in her own eyes and those of the Egyptians Antony held this position—had been induced to wed his sister, Octavia, and thereby stamp her, Cleopatra, as merely his love, cast a doubt upon the legitimate birth of her children; of the false friend of the trusting Antony who, before the battle of Actium, had most deeply humiliated and insulted both!

On the contrary, her royal pride rebelled against obeying the command of such a man to commit the most atrocious deed; and from childhood this pride had been as much a part of her nature as her breath and the pulsation of her heart. And yet, for her children's sake, she might perhaps have incurred this disgrace, had it not been at the same time the grave of the best and noblest things which she desired to implant in the young souls of the twins and Alexander.

While thinking of the children's curses she had risen from her seat. Why should she reflect and consider longer? She had found the clear perception she sought. Let Gorgias hasten the building of the tomb. Should Fate demand her life, she would not resist if she were permitted to preserve it only at the cost of murder or base treachery. Her lover's was already forfeited. At his side she had enjoyed a radiant, glowing, peerless bliss, of which the world still talked with envious amazement. At his side, when all was over, she would rest in the grave, and compel the world to remember with respectful sympathy the royal lovers, Antony and Cleopatra. Her children should be able to think of her with untroubled hearts, and not even the shadow of a bitter feeling, a warning thought, should deter them from adorning their parents' grave with flowers, weeping at its foot, invoking and offering sacrifices to their spirits.

Then she glanced at the statue of Berenike, who had also once worn on her brow the double crown of Egypt. She, too, had early died a violent death; she, too, had known how to love. The vow to sacrifice her beautiful hair to Aphrodite if her husband returned uninjured from the Syrian war had rendered her name illustrious. "Berenike's Hair" was still to be seen as a constellation in the night heavens.

Though this woman had sinned often and heavily, one act of loyal love had made her an honoured, worshipped princess. She—Cleopatra—would do something still greater. The sacrifice which she intended to impose upon herself would weigh far more heavily in the balance than a handful of beautiful tresses, and would comprise sovereignty and life.

With head erect and a sense of proud self-reliance she gazed at the noble marble countenance of the Cyrenian queen. Ere entering the sanctuary she had imagined that she knew how the criminals whom she had sentenced to death must feel. Now that she herself had done with life, she felt as if she were relieved from a heavy burden, and yet her heart ached, and—especially when she thought of her children—she was overwhelmed with the emotion which is the most painful of all forms of compassion—pity for herself.

CHAPTER XVIII.

WHEN Cleopatra left the temple, Iras marvelled at the change in her appearance. The severe tension which had given her beautiful face a shade of harshness had yielded to an expression of gentle sadness that enhanced its charm, yet her features quickly brightened as her attendant pointed to the procession which was just entering the forecourt of the palace.

In Alexandria and throughout Egypt birthdays were celebrated as far as possible. Therefore, to do honour to the twins, the children of the city had been sent to offer their congratulations, and at the same time to assure their royal mother of the love and devotion of the citizens.

The return to the palace occupied only a few minutes, and as Cleopatra, hastily donning festal garments, gazed down at the bands of children, it seemed as if Fate by this fair spectacle had given her a sign of approval of her design.

She was soon standing hand in hand with the twins upon the balcony before which the procession had halted. Hundreds of boys and girls of the same age as the prince and princess had flocked thither, the former bearing bouquets, the latter small baskets filled with lilies and roses. Every head was crowned with a wreath, and many of the girls wore garlands of flowers. A chorus of youths and maidens sang a festal hymn, beseeching the gods to grant the royal mother and children every happiness; the leader of the chorus of girls made a short address in the name of the city, and during this speech the children formed in ranks, the tallest in the rear, the smallest in the front, and the others between according to their height. The scene resembled a living garden, in which rosy faces were the beautiful flowers.

Cleopatra thanked the citizens for the charming greeting sent to her by those whom they held dearest, and assured them that she returned their love. Her eyes grew dim with tears as she went with her three children to the throng who offered their congratulations, and an unusually pretty little girl whom she kissed threw her arms around her as tenderly as if she were her own mother. And how beautiful was the scene when the girls strewed the contents of their little baskets on the ground before her, and the boys, with many a ringing shout and loving wish, offered the bouquets to her and the twins!

Charmian had not forgotten to provide the gifts; and when the chamberlains and waiting-women led the children into a large hall to offer them refreshments, the Queen's eyes sparkled so brightly that the companion of her childhood ventured to make her difficult confession.

And, as so often happens, the event we most dread shows, when it actually occurs, a friendly or indifferent aspect; this was the case now. Nothing in life is either great or small—the one may be transformed to the other, according to the things with which it is compared. The tallest man becomes a dwarf beside a rocky giant of the mountain chain, the smallest is a Titan to the swarming ants in the forest. The beggar seizes as a treasure what the rich man scornfully casts aside. That which the day before yesterday seemed to Cleopatra unendurable, roused her keenest anxiety, robbed her of part of her night's repose, and induced her to adopt strenuous measures, now appeared trivial, and scarcely worthy of consideration.

Yesterday and to-day had brought events and called up questions which forced Barine's disappearance into the realm of unimportant matters.

Charmian's confession was preceded by the statement that she longed for rest yet, nevertheless, was ready to remain with her royal friend, in every situation, until she no longer desired her services and sent her away. But she feared that this moment had come.

Cleopatra interrupted her with the assurance that she was speaking of something utterly impossible; and when Charmian disclosed Barine's escape, and admitted that it was she who had aided the flight of the innocent and sorely threatened granddaughter of Didymus, the Queen started up angrily and frowned, but it was only for a moment. Then, with a smile, she shook her finger at her friend, embraced her, and gravely but kindly assured her that, of all vices, ingratitude was most alien to her nature. The companion of her childhood had bestowed so many proofs of faithfulness, love, self-sacrifice, and laborious service in her behalf that they could not be long outweighed by a single act of wilful disobedience. An abundant supply would still remain, by virtue of which she might continue to sin without fearing that Cleopatra would ever part from her Charmian.

The latter again perceived that nothing on earth could be hostile or sharp enough to sever the bond which united her to this woman. When her lips overflowed with the gratitude which filled her heart, Cleopatra admitted that it seemed as if, in aiding Barine's escape, she had rendered her a service. The caution with which Charmian had concealed Barine's refuge had not escaped her notice, and she did not ask to learn it. It was enough for her that the dangerous beauty was out of Cæsarion's reach. As for Antony, a wall now separated him from the world, and consequently from the woman who, spite of Alexas's accusations, had probably never stood closer to his heart.

Charmian now eagerly strove to show the

Queen what had induced the Syrian to pursue Barine so vindictively. It was evident—and scarcely needed proof—that Mark Antony's whole acquaintanceship with the old scholar's granddaughter had been far from leading to any tender relation. But Cleopatra gave only partial attention. The man whom she had loved with every pulsation of her heart already seemed to her only a dear memory. She did not forget the happiness enjoyed with and through him, or the wrong she had done by the use of the magic goblet; yet with the wall on the Choma, which divided him from her and the rest of the world, and her command to have the mausoleum built, she imagined that the season of love was over. Any new additions to this chapter of the life of her heart were but the close. Even the jealousy which had clouded the happiness of her love like a fleeting, rapidly changing shadow, she believed she had now renounced forever.

While Charmian protested that no one save Dion had ever been heard with favour by Barine, and related many incidents of her former life, Cleopatra's thoughts were with Antony. Like the image of the beloved dead, the towering figure of the Roman hero rose before her mind, but she recalled him only as he was prior to the battle of Actium. She desired and expected nothing more from the broken-spirited man, whose condition was perhaps her own fault. But she had resolved to atone for her guilt, and would do so at the cost of throne and life. This settled the account. Whatever her remaining span of existence might add or subtract, was part of the bargain.

The entrance of Alexas interrupted her. With fiery passion he expressed his regret that he had been defrauded by base intrigues of the right bestowed upon him to pass sentence upon a guilty woman. This was the more difficult to bear because he was deprived of the possibility of providing for the pursuit of the fugitive. Antony had honoured him with the commission to win Herod back to his cause. He was to leave Alexandria that very night. As nothing could be expected in this matter from the misanthropic Imperator, he hoped that the Queen would avenge such an offence to her dignity, and adopt severe measures towards the singer and her last lover, Dion, who with sacrilegious hands had wounded the son of Cæsar.

But Cleopatra, with royal dignity, kept him within the limits of his position, commanded him not to mention the affair to her again, and then, with a sorrowful smile, wished him success with Herod, in whose return to the lost cause of Antony, however, much as she prized the skill of the mediator, she did not believe.

When he had retired, she exclaimed to Charmian: "Was I blind? This man is a traitor! We shall discover it. Wherever Dion has taken his young wife, let her be carefully concealed, not from me, but from this Syrian. It is easier to defend one's self against the lion than the scorpion. You, my friend, will see that Archibius seeks me this very day. I must talk with him, and—you no longer have any thought of a parting? Another will come soon enough, which will forever forbid these lips from kissing your dear face."

As she spoke, she again clasped the companion of her childhood in her arms, and when Iras entered to request an audience for Lucilius, Antony's most faithful friend, Cleopatra, who had noticed the younger woman's envious glance at the embrace, said: "Was I mistaken in fancying that you imagined yourself slighted for Charmian, who is an older friend? That would be wrong; for I love and need you both. You are her niece, and indebted to her for much kindness from your earliest childhood. So, even though you will lose the joy of revenge upon a hated enemy, forget what has happened, as I did, and maintain your former affectionate companionship. I will reward you for it with the only thing that the daughter of the wealthy Krates cannot purchase, yet which she probably rates at no low value—the love of her royal friend."

With these words she clasped Iras also in a close embrace, and when the latter left the room to summon Lucilius, she thought: "No woman has ever won so much love; perhaps that is why she possesses so great a treasure of it, and can afford such unspeakable happiness by its bestowal. Or is she so much beloved because she entered the world full of its wealth, and dispenses it as the sun diffuses light? Surely that must be the case. I have reason to believe it, for whom did I ever love save the Queen? No one, not even myself, and I know no one in whose love for me I can believe. But why did Dion, whom I loved so fervently, disdain me? Fool! Why did Mark Antony prefer Cleopatra to Octavia, who was not less fair, whose heart was his, and whose hand held the sovereignty of half the world?"

Passing on as she spoke, she soon returned, ushering the Roman Lucilius into the presence of the Queen. A gallant deed had bound this man to Antony. After the battle of Philippi, when the army of the republicans fled, Brutus had been on the point of being seized by the enemy's horsemen; but Lucilius, at the risk of being cut down, had personated him, and thereby, though but for a short time, rescued him. This had seemed to Antony unusual and noble and, in his generous manner, he had not only forgiven him, but bestowed his favour upon him. Lucilius was grateful, and gave him the same fidelity he had showed to Brutus. At Actium he had risked Antony's favour to prevent his deserting Cleopatra after the battle, and then accompanied him in his flight. Now he was bearing him company in his seclusion on the Choma.

The grey-haired man who, but a short time before, had retained all the vigour of youth, approached the Queen with bowed head and saddened heart. His face, so regular in its contours, had undergone a marked change within the past few weeks. The cheeks were sunken, the features had grown sharper, and there was a sorrowful expression in the eyes, which, when informing Cleopatra of his friend's condition, glittered with tears.

Before the hapless battle he was one of Cleopatra's most enthusiastic admirers; but since he had been forced to see his friend and benefactor risk fame, happiness, and honour to follow the Queen, he had cherished a feeling of bitter resentment towards her. He would certainly have spared himself this mission, had he not been sure that she who had brought her lover to ruin was the only person who could rouse him from spiritless languor to fresh energy and interest in life.

From motives of friendship, urged by no one, he came unbidden to the woman whom he had formerly so sincerely admired, to entreat her to cheer the unfortunate man, rouse him, and remind him of his duty. He had little news to impart; for on the voyage she had herself witnessed long enough the pitiable condition of her husband. Now Antony was beginning to be content in it, and this was what most sorely troubled the faithful friend.

The Imperator had called the little palace which he occupied on the Choma his Timonium, because he compared himself with the famous Athenian misanthrope who, after fortune abandoned him, had also been betrayed by many of his former friends. Even at Tænarum he had thought of returning to the Choma, and by means of a wall, which would separate it from the mainland, rendering it as inaccessible as—according to rumour—the grave of Timon at Halæ near Athens. Gorgias had erected it, and whoever wished to visit the hermit was forced to go by sea and request admittance, which was granted to few.

Cleopatra listened to Lucilius with sympathy, and then asked whether there was no way of cheering or comforting the wretched man.

"No, your Majesty," he replied. "His favourite occupation is to recall what he once possessed, but only to show the uselessness of these memories. 'What joys has life not offered me?' he asks, and then adds: 'But they were repeated again and again, and after being enjoyed for the tenth time they became monotonous and lost their charm. Then they caused satiety to the verge of loathing.' Only necessary things, such as bread and water, he says, possess real value; but he desires neither, because he has even less taste for them than for the dainties which spoil a man's morrow. Yesterday, in a specially gloomy hour, he spoke of gold. This was perhaps most worthy of desire. The mere sight of it awakened pleasant hopes, because it might afford so many gratifications. Then he laughed bitterly, exclaiming that those joys were the very ones which produced the most disagreeable satiety. Even gold was not worth the trouble of stretching out one's hand.

"He is fond of enlarging upon such fancies, and finds images to make his meaning clear.

"'In the snow upon the highest mountain-peak the feet grow cold,' he said. 'In the mire they are warm, but the dark mud is ugly and clings to them.'

"Then I remarked that between the morass and the mountain-snows lie sunny valleys where life would be pleasant; but he flew into a rage, vehemently protesting that he would never be content with the pitiable middle course of Horace. Then he exclaimed: 'Ay, I am vanquished. Octavianus and his Agrippa are the conquerors; but if a rock mutilates or an elephant's clumsy foot crushes me, I am nevertheless of a higher quality than either.'"

"There spoke the old Mark Antony!" cried Cleopatra; but again Lucilius's loyal heart throbbed with resentment against the woman who had fostered the recklessness which had brought his powerful friend to ruin, and he continued:

"But he often sees himself in a different light.

'No writer could invent a more unworthy life than mine,' he exclaimed recently. 'A farce ending in a tragedy.'"

Lucilius might have added still harsher sayings, but the sorrowful expression in the tearful eyes of the afflicted Queen silenced them upon his lips.

Yet Cleopatra's name blended with most of the words uttered by the broken-spirited man. Sometimes it was associated with the most furious reproaches, but more frequently with expressions of boundless delight and wild outbursts of fervent longing, and this was what inspired Lucilius with the hope that the Queen's influence would be effectual with his friend. Therefore he repeated some especially ardent words, to which Cleopatra listened with grateful joy.

Yet, when Lucilius paused, she remarked that doubtless the misanthropist had spoken of her, and probably of Octavia also, in quite a different way. She was prepared for the worst, for she was one of the rocks against which his greatness had been shattered.

This reminded Lucilius of the comment Antony had made upon the three women whom he had wedded, and he answered reluctantly: "Fulvia, the wife of his youth—I knew the bold, hot-blooded woman, the former wife of Clodius—he called the tempest which swelled his sails."

"Yes, yes!" cried Cleopatra. "So she did. He owes her much; but I, too, am indebted to the dead Fulvia. She taught him to recognize and yield to woman's power."

"Not always to his advantage," retorted Lucilius, whose resentment was revived by the last sentence and, without heeding the faint flush on the Queen's cheek, he added: "Of Octavia he said that she was the straight path which leads to happiness, and those who are content to walk in it are acceptable to gods and men."

"Then why did he not suffer it to content him?" cried Cleopatra wrathfully.

"Fulvia's school," replied the Roman, "was probably the last where he would learn the moderation which—as you know—is so alien to his nature. His opinion of the quiet valleys and middle course you have just heard."

"'But I, what have *I* been to him?" urged the Queen.

Lucilius bent his gaze for a short time on the floor, then answered hesitatingly:

"You asked to hear, and the Queen's command must be obeyed. He compared your Majesty to a delicious banquet given to celebrate a victory, at which the guests, crowned with garlands, revel *before* the battle——"

"Which is lost," said the Queen hurriedly, in a muffled voice. "The comparison is apt. Now, after the defeat, it would be absurd to prepare another feast. The tragedy is closing, so the play (doubtless he said so) which preceded it would be but a wearisome repetition if performed a second time. One thing, it is true, seems desirable—a closing act of reconciliation. If you think it is in my power to recall my husband to active life, rely upon me. The banquet of which he spoke occupied long years. The dessert will consume little time, but I am ready to serve it. When I asked permission to visit him he refused. What plan of meeting have you arranged?"

"That I will leave to your feminine delicacy of feeling," replied Lucilius. "Yet I have come with a request whose fulfilment will perhaps contain the answer. Eros, Mark Antony's faithful body-slave, humbly petitions your Majesty to grant him a few minutes' audience. You know the worthy fellow. He would die for you and his master, and he—I once heard from your lips the remark of King Antiochus, that no man was great to his body-slave—thus Eros sees his master's weaknesses and lofty qualities from a nearer point of view than we, and he is shrewd. Antony gave him his freedom long ago, and if your Majesty does not object to receiving a man so low in station——"

"Let him come," replied Cleopatra. "Your demand upon me is just. Unhappily, I am but too well aware of the atonement due your friend. Before you came, I was engaged in making preparations for the fulfilment of one of his warmest wishes."

With these words she dismissed the Roman. Her feelings as she watched his departure were of very mingled character. The yearning for the happiness of which she had been so long deprived had again awaked, while the unkind words which he had applied to her still rankled in her heart. But the door had scarcely closed behind Lucilius when the usher announced a deputation of the members of the museum.

The learned gentlemen came to complain of the wrong which had been done to their colleague, Didymus, and also to express their loyalty during these trying times. Cleopatra assured them of her favour, and said that she had already offered ample compensation to the old philosopher. In a certain sense she was one of themselves. They all knew that, from early youth, she had honoured and shared their labours. In proof of this, she would present to the library of the museum the two hundred thousand volumes from Pergamus, one of the most valuable gifts Mark Antony had ever bestowed upon her, and which she had hitherto regarded merely as a loan. This she hoped would repay Didymus for the injury which, to her deep regret, had been inflicted upon him, and at least partially repair the loss sustained by the former library of the museum during the conflagration in the Bruchium.

The sages, eagerly assuring her of their gratitude and devotion, retired. Most of them were personally known to Cleopatra who, to their mutual pleasure and advantage, had measured her intellectual powers with the most brilliant minds of their body.

The sun had already set, when a procession of the priests of Serapis, the chief god of the city, whose coming had been announced the day before, appeared at Lochias. Accompanied by torch and lantern bearers, it moved forward with slow and solemn majesty. In harmony with the nature of Serapis, there were many reminders of death.

The meaning of every image, every standard, every shrine, every peculiarity of the music and singing, was familiar to the Queen. Even the changing colours of the lights referred to the course of growth and decay in the universe and in human life, and the magnificent close of the chant of homage which represented the reception of the royal soul into the essence of the deity, the apotheosis of the sovereign, was well suited to stir the heart; for a sea of light unexpectedly flooded the whole procession and, while its glow irradiated the huge pile of the palace, the sea with its forest of ships and masts, and the shore with its temples, pylons, obelisks, and superb buildings, all the choruses, accompanied by the music of sackbuts, cymbals, and lutes, blended in a mighty hymn, whose waves of sound rose to the star-strewn sky and reached the open sea beyond the Pharos.

Many a symbolical image suggested death and

the resurrection, defeat and a victory following it by the aid of great Serapis; and when the torches retired, vanishing in the darkness, with the last notes of the chanting of the priests, Cleopatra raised her head, feeling as if the vow she had made during the gloomy singing of the aged men and the extinguishing of the torches had received the approval of the deity brought by her forefathers to Alexandria and enthroned there to unite in his own person the nature of the Greek and the Egyptian gods.

Her tomb was to be built and, if destiny was fulfilled, to receive her lover and herself. She had perceived from Antony's bitter words, as well as the looks and tones of Lucilius, that he, as well as the man to whom her heart still clung with indissoluble bonds, held her responsible for Actium and the fall of his greatness.

The world, she knew, would imitate them, but it should learn that if love had robbed the greatest man of his day of fame and sovereignty, that love had been worthy of the highest price.

The belief which had just been symbolically represented to her—that it was allotted to the vanishing light to rise again in new and radiant splendour—she would maintain for the present, though the best success could scarcely lead to anything more than merely fanning the glimmering spark and deferring its extinction.

For herself there was no longer any great victory to win which would be worth the conflict. Yet the weapons must not rest until the end. Antony must not perish, growling, like a second Timon, or a wild beast caught in a snare. She would rekindle, though but for the last blaze, the fire of his hero-nature, which blind love for her and the magic spell that had enabled her to bind his will had covered for a time with ashes.

While listening to the resurrection hymn of the priests of Serapis, she had asked herself if it might not be possible to give Antony, when he had been roused to fresh energy, the son of Cæsar as a companion in arms. True, she had found the boy in a mood far different from the one for which she had hoped. If he had once been carried on to a bold deed, it seemed to have exhausted his energy; for he remained absorbed in the most pitiable love-sickness. Yet he had not recovered from his illness. When he was better he would surely wake to active interest in the events which threatened to exert so great an influence on his own existence and, like the humblest slave, lament the defeat of Actium. Hitherto he had listened to the tidings of battle which had reached his ears with an indifference that seemed intelligible and pardonable only when attributed to his wound.

His tutor Rhodon had just requested a leave of absence, remarking that Cæsarion would not lack companions, since he was expecting Antyllus and other youths of his own age. A flood of light streamed from the windows of the reception hall of the "King of kings." There was still time to seek him and make him understand what was at stake. Ah! if she could but succeed in awaking his father's spirit! If that culpable attack should prove the harbinger of future deeds of manly daring!

No interview with him as yet had encouraged this expectation, but a mother's heart easily sees, even in disappointment, a step which leads to a new hope. When Charmian entered to announce Antony's body-slave, she sent word to him to wait, and requested her friend to accompany her to her son.

As they approached the apartments occupied by Cæsarion, Antyllus's loud voice reached them through the open door, whose curtain was only half drawn. The first word which the Queen distinguished was her own name; so, motioning to her companion, she stood still. Barine was again the subject of conversation.

Antony's son was relating what Alexas had told him. Cleopatra, the Syrian had asserted, intended to send the young beauty to the mines or into exile, and severely punish Dion; but both had made their escape. The Ephebi had behaved treacherously by taking sides with their foe. But this was because they were not yet invested with their robes. He hoped to induce his father to do this as soon as he shook off his pitiable misanthropy. And he must also be persuaded to direct the pursuit of the fugitives. "This will not be difficult," he cried insolently, "for the old man appreciates beauty, and has himself cast an eye on the singer. If they capture her, I'll guarantee nothing, you 'King of kings!' for, spite of his grey beard, he can cut us all out with the women, and Barine—as we have heard—doesn't think a man of much importance until his locks begin to grow thin. I gave Derketæus orders to send all his men in pursuit. He's as cunning as a fox, and the police are compelled to obey him."

"If I were not forced to lie here like a dead donkey, I would soon find her," sighed Cæsarion. "Night or day, she is never out of my mind. I have already spent everything I possessed in the search. Yesterday I sent for the steward Seleukus. What is the use of being my mother's son, and the fat little fellow isn't specially scrupulous! He will do nothing, yet there must be gold enough. The Queen has sunk millions in the sand on the Syrian frontier of the Delta. There is to be a square hole or something of the sort dug there to hide the fleet. I only half understand the absurd plan. The money might have paid hundreds of spies. So talents are thrown away, and the strong-box is locked against the son. But I'll find one that will open to me. I must have her, though I risk the crown. It always sounds like a jeer when they call me the King of kings. I am not fit for sovereignty. Besides, the throne will be seized ere I really ascend it. We are conquered, and if we succeed in concluding a peace, which will secure us life and a little more, we must be content. For my part, I shall be satisfied with a country estate on the water, a sufficient supply of money and, above all, Barine. What do I care for Egypt? As Cæsar's son I ought to have ruled Rome; but the immortals knew what they were doing when they prompted my father to disinherit me. To govern the world one must have less need of sleep. Really—you know it—I always feel tired, even when I am well. People must let me alone! Your father, too, Antyllus, is laying down his arms and letting things go as they will."

"Ah, so he is!" cried Antony's son indignantly. "But just wait! The sleeping lion will wake again, and, when he uses his teeth and paws——"

"My mother will run away, and your father will follow her," replied Cæsarion with a melancholy smile, wholly untinged by scorn. "All is lost. But conquered kings and queens are permitted to live. Cæsar's son will not be exhibited to the Quirites in the triumphal procession. Rhodon says that there would be an insurrection if I appeared in the Forum. If I go there again, it certainly will not be in Octavianus's train. I am not suited for that kind of ignominy. It would stifle me and, ere I would grant any man the pleasure of dragging the son of Cæsar behind him to increase his own renown, I would put an end ten, nay, a hundred times over, in the good old Roman fashion, to my life, which is by no means especially attractive. What is sweeter than sound sleep, and who will disturb and rouse me when Death has lowered his torch before me? But now I think I shall be spared this extreme. Whatever else they may inflict upon me will scarcely exceed my powers of endurance. If any one has learned contentment it is I. The King of kings and Co-Regent of the Great Queen has been trained persistently, and with excellent success, to be content. What should I be, and what *am* I? Yet I do not complain, and wish to accuse no one. We need not summon Octavianus, and when he is here let him take what he will if he only spares the lives of my mother, the twins, and little Alexander, whom I love, and bestows on me the estate—the main thing is that it must be full of fishponds—of which I spoke. The private citizen Cæsarion, who devotes his time to fishing and the books he likes to read, will gladly be allowed to choose a wife to suit his own taste. The more humble her origin, the more easily I shall win the consent of the Roman guardian."

"Do you know, Cæsarion," interrupted Antony's unruly son, leaning back on the cushions and stretching his feet farther in front of him, "if you were not the King of kings I should be inclined to call you a base, mean-natured fellow! One who has the good fortune to be the son of Julius Cæsar ought not to forget it so disgracefully. My gall overflows at your whimpering. By the dog! It was one of my most senseless pranks to take you to the singer. I should think there would be other things to occupy the mind of the King of kings. Besides, Barine cares no more for you than the last fish you caught. She showed that plainly enough. I say once more, if Derketæus's men succeed in capturing the beauty who has robbed you of your senses, she won't go with you to your miserable estate to cook the fish you catch, for if we have her again, and my father holds out his hand to her, all your labour will be in vain. He saw the fair enchantress only twice, and had no time to become better acquainted, but she captured his fancy and, if I remind him of her, who knows what will happen?"

Here Cleopatra beckoned to her companion and returned to her apartments with drooping head. On reaching them, she broke the silence, saying: "Listening, Charmian, is unworthy of a Queen; but if all listeners heard things so painful, one need no longer guard keyholes and chinks of doors. I must recover my calmness ere I receive Eros. One thing more. Is Barine's hiding-place secure?"

"I don't know—Archibius says so."

"Very well. They are searching for her zealously enough, as you heard, and she must not be found. I am glad that she did not set a snare for the boy. How a jealous heart leads us astray! Were she here, I would grant her anything to make amends for my unjust suspicion of her and Antony. And to think that Alexas—but for your interposition he would have succeeded—meant to send her to the mines! It is a terrible warning to be on my guard. Against whom? First of all, my own weakness. This is a day of recognition. A noble aim, but on the way the feet bleed, and the heart—ah! Charmian, the poor, weak, disappointed heart!"

She sighed heavily, and supported her head on the arm resting upon the table at her side. The polished, exquisitely grained surface of thya-wood was worth a large estate; the gems in the rings and bracelets which glittered on her hand and arm would have purchased a principality. This thought entered her mind and, overpowered by a feeling of angry disgust, she would fain have cast all the costly rubbish into the sea or the destroying flames.

She would gladly have been a beggar, content with the barley bread of Epicurus, she said to herself, if in return she could but have inspired her son even with the views of the reckless blusterer Antyllus. Her worst fears had not pictured Cæsarion so weak, so insignificant. She could no longer rest upon her cushions; and while, with drooping head, she gazed backward over the past, the accusing voice in her own breast cried out that she was reaping what she had sowed. She had repressed, curbed the boy's awakening will to secure his obedience; understood how to prevent any exercise of his ability or efforts in wider circles.

True, it had been done on many a pretext. Why should not her son taste the quiet happiness which she had enjoyed in the garden of Epicurus? And was not the requirement that whoever is to command must first learn to obey, based upon old experiences?

But this was a day of reckoning and insight, and for the first time she found courage to confess that her own burning ambition had marked out the course of Cæsarion's education. She had not repressed his talents from cool calculation, but it had been pleasant to her to see him grow up free from aspirations. She had granted the dreamer repose without arousing him. How often she had rejoiced over the certainty that this son, on whom Antony, after his victory over the Parthians, had bestowed the title of Co-Regent, would never rebel against his mother's guardianship! The welfare of the state had doubtless been better secured in her trained hands than in those of an inexperienced boy. And the proud consciousness of power! Her heart swelled. So long as she lived she would remain Queen. To transfer the sovereignty to another, whatever name he might bear, had seemed to her impossible. Now she knew how little her son yearned for lofty things. Her heart contracted. The saying " You reap what you sowed " gave her no peace, and wherever she turned in her past life she perceived the fruit of the seeds which she had buried in the ground. The field was sinking under the burden of the ears of misfortune. The harvest was ripe for the reaper; but, ere he raised the sickle, the owner's claim must be preserved. Gorgias must hasten the building of the tomb; the end could not be long deferred. How to shape this worthily, if the victor left her no other choice, had just been pointed out by the son of whom she was ashamed. His father's noble blood forbade him to bear the deepest ignominy with the patience his mother had inculcated.

It had grown late ere she admitted Antony's body-slave, but for her the business of the night was just commencing. After he had gone she would be engaged for hours with the commanders of the army, the fleet, the fortifications. The soliciting of allies, too, must be carried on by means of letters containing the most stirring appeals to the heart.

Eros, Antony's body-slave, appeared. His kind eyes filled with tears at the sight of the Queen. Grief had not lessened the roundness of his handsome face, but the expression of mischievous, often insolent, gaiety had given place to a sorrowful droop of the lips, and his fair hair had begun to turn grey.

Lucilius's information that Cleopatra had consented to make advances to Antony had seemed like the rising of the sun after a long period of darkness. In his eyes, not only his master, but everything else, must yield to the power of the Queen. He had heard Antony at Tarsus inveigh against "the Egyptian serpent," protesting that he would make her pay so dearly for her questionable conduct towards himself and the cause of Cæsar that the treasure-houses on the Nile should be like an empty wine-skin; yet, a few hours after, body and soul had been in her toils. So it had continued till the battle of Actium. Now there was nothing more to lose; but what might not Cleopatra bestow upon his master? He thought of the delightful years during which his face had grown so round, and every day fresh pleasures and spectacles, such as the world would never again witness, had satiated eye and ear, palate and nostril, —nay, even curiosity. If they could be repeated, even in a simpler form, so much the better. His main—nay, almost his sole—desire was to release his lord from this wretched solitude, this horrible misanthropy, so ill suited to his nature.

Cleopatra had kept him waiting two hours, but he would willingly have loitered in the anteroom thrice as long if she only determined to follow his counsel. It was worth considering, and Eros did not hesitate to give it. No one could foresee how Antony would greet Cleopatra herself, so he proposed that she should send Charmian—not alone, but with her clever hunch-backed maid, to whom the Imperator himself had given the name "Aisopion." He liked Charmian, and could never see the dusky maid without jesting with her. If his master could once be induced to show a cheerful face to others besides himself, Eros, and perceived how much better it was to laugh than to lapse into sullen reverie and anger, much would be gained, and Charmian would do the rest, if she brought a loving message from her royal mistress.

Hitherto Cleopatra had not interrupted him; but when she expressed the opinion that a slave's nimble tongue would have little power to change the deep despondency of a man overwhelmed by the most terrible disaster, Eros waved his short, broad hand, saying:

"I trust your Majesty will pardon the frankness of a man so humble in degree, but those in high station often permit us to see what they hide from one another. Only the loftiest and the lowliest, the gods and the slaves, behold the great without disguise. May my ears be cropped if the Imperator's melancholy and misanthropy are so intense! All this is a disguise which pleases him. You know how, in better days, he enjoyed appearing as Dionysus, and with what wanton gaiety he played the part of the god. Now he is hiding his real, cheerful face behind the mask of unsocial melancholy, because he thinks the former does not suit this time of misfortune. True, he often says things which make your skin creep, and frequently broods mournfully over his own thoughts. But this never lasts long when we are alone. If I come in with a very funny story, and he doesn't silence me at once, you can rely on his surpassing it with a still more comical one. A short time ago I reminded him of the fishing party when your Majesty had a diver fasten a salted herring on his hook. You ought to have heard him laugh, and exclaim what happy days those were. The lady Charmian need only remind him of them, and Aisopion spice the allusion with a jest. I'll give my nose—true, it's only a small one, but everybody values that feature most—if they don't persuade him to leave that horrible crow's nest in the middle of the sea. They must remind him of the twins and little Alexander; for when he permits me to talk about them his brow smooths most speedily. He still speaks very often to Lucilius and his other friends of his great plans of forming a powerful empire in the East, with Alexandria as its principal city. His warrior blood is not yet calm. A short time ago I was even ordered to sharpen the curved Persian scimitar he likes to wield. One could not know what service it might be, he said. Then he swung his mighty arm. By the dog! The grey-haired giant still has the strength of three youths. When he is once more with you, among warriors and battle chargers, all will be well."

"Let us hope so," replied Cleopatra kindly, and promised to follow his advice.

When Iras, who had taken Charmian's place, accompanied the Queen to her chamber after several hours of toil, she found her silent and sad. Lost in thought, she accepted her attendant's aid, breaking her silence only after she had gone to her couch. "This has been a hard day, Iras," she said; "it brought nothing save the confirmation of an old saying, perhaps the most ancient in the world: 'Every one will reap only what he sows. The plant which grows from the seed you place in the earth may be crushed, but no power in the world will compel the seed to develop differently or produce fruit unlike what Nature has assigned to it.' My seed was evil. This now appears in the time of harvest. But we will yet bring a handful of good wheat to the storehouses. We will provide for that while there is time. I will talk with Gorgias early to-morrow morning. While we were building, you showed good taste and often suggested new ideas. When Gorgias brings the plans for the mausoleum you shall examine them with me. You have a right to do so, for, if I am not mistaken, few will visit the finished structure more frequently than my Iras."

The girl started up and, raising her hand as if taking a vow, exclaimed: "Your tomb will vainly wait my visit; your end will be mine also.

"May the gods preserve your youth from it!" replied the Queen in a tone of grave remonstrance. "We still live and will do battle."

CHAPTER XIX.

NIGHT brought little sleep to Cleopatra. Memory followed memory, plan was added to plan. The resolve made the day before was the right one. To-day she would begin its execution. Whatever might happen, she was prepared for every contingency.

Ere she went to her work she granted a second audience to the Roman envoy. Timagenes exerted all his powers of eloquence, skill in persuasion, wit, and ingenuity. He again promised to Cleopatra life and liberty, and to her children the throne; but when he insisted upon the surrender or death of Mark Antony as the first condition of any further negotiations, Cleopatra remained steadfast, and the ambassador set forth on his way home without any pledge.

After he had gone, the Queen and Iras looked over the plans for the tomb brought by Gorgias, but the intense agitation of her soul distracted Cleopatra's attention, and she begged him to come again at a later hour. When she was alone, she took out the letters which Cæsar and Antony had written to her. How acute, subtle, and tender were those of the former; how ardent, impassioned, yet sincere were those of the mighty and fiery orator, whose eloquence swept the listening multitudes with him, yet whom her little hand had drawn wherever she desired!

Her heart throbbed faster when she thought of the meeting with Antony, now close at hand; for Charmian had gone with the Nubian to invite him to join her again. They had started several hours ago, and she awaited their return with increasing impatience. She had summoned him for their last mutual battle. That he would come she did not doubt. But could she succeed in rekindling his courage? Two persons so closely allied should sink and perish, still firmly united, in the final battle, if victory was denied.

Archibius was now announced.

It soothed her merely to gaze into the faithful countenance, which recalled so many of her happiest memories.

She opened her whole soul to him without reserve, and he drew himself up to his full height, as if restored to youth; while when she told him that she would never sully herself by treachery to her lover and husband, and had resolved to die worthy of her name, the expression of his eyes revealed that she had chosen the right path.

Ere she had made the request that he should undertake the education and guidance of the children, he voluntarily proposed to devote his best powers to them. The plan of uniting Didymus's garden with the Lochias and giving it to the little ones also met with his approval. His sister had already told him that Cleopatra had determined to build her tomb. He hoped, he added, that its doors would not open to her for many years.

She shook her head sorrowfully, exclaiming: "Would that I could read every face as I do yours! My friend Archibius wishes me a long life, if any one does; but he is as wise as he is faithful, and therefore will consider that earthly life is by no means a boon in every case. Besides, he says to himself: 'Events are impending over this Queen and woman, my friend, which will perhaps render it advisable to make use of the great privilege which the immortals bestow on human beings when it becomes desirable for them to leave the stage of life. So let her build her tomb.' Have I read the old familiar book aright?"

"On the whole, yes," he answered gravely. "But it is inscribed upon its pages that a great princess and faithful mother can be permitted to set forth on the last journey, whence there is no return, only when——"

"When," she interrupted, "a shameful end threatens to fall upon the fair beginning and brilliant middle period, as a swarm of locusts darkens the air and devours and devastates the fields. I know it, and will act accordingly."

"And," added Archibius, "this end also (faithful to your nature) you will shape regally. On my way here I met my sister near the Choma. You sent her to your husband. He will grasp the proffered hand. Now that it is necessary to stake everything or surrender, the grandson of Herakles will again display his former heroic power. Perhaps, stimulated and encouraged by the example of the woman he loves, he will even force hostile Fate to show him fresh favour."

"Destiny will pursue its course," interrupted Cleopatra firmly. "But Antony must help me to heap fresh obstacles in the pathway, and when he wishes to use his giant strength, what masses of rock his mighty arm can hurl!"

"And if your lofty spirit smooths the path for him, then, my royal mistress——"

"Even then the close of the tragedy will be death, and every scene a disappointment. Was not the plan of bringing the fleet across the isthmus bold and full of promise? Even the professional engineers greeted it with applause, and yet it proved impracticable. Destiny dug its grave. And the terrible omens before and after Actium, and the stars—the stars! Everything points to speedy destruction, everything! Every hour brings news of the desertion of some prince or general. As if from a watch-tower, I now overlook what is growing from the seed I sowed. Sterile ears or poisonous vegetation, wherever I turn my eyes. And yet!

You, who know my life from its beginning, tell me—must I veil my head in shame when the question is asked, what powers of intellect, what talents, industry, and desire for good Cleopatra displayed?"

"No, my royal mistress, a thousand times no!"

"Yet the fruit of every tree I planted degenerated and decayed. Cæsarion is withering in the flower of his youth—by whose fault I know only too well. You will now take charge of the education of the other children. So it is for you to consider what brought me where I now stand, and how to guard their life-bark from wandering and shipwreck."

"Let me train them to be human beings," replied Archibius gravely, "and preserve them from the desire to enter the lists with the gods. From the simple Cleopatra in the garden of Epicurus, who was a delight to the good and wise, you became the 'new Isis,' to whom the multitude raised hearts, eyes, and hands, dazzled and blinded. We will transfer the twins, Helios and Selene, the sun and the moon, from heaven to earth; they must become mortals—Greeks. I will not transplant them to the garden of Epicurus, but to another, where the air is more bracing. The inscription on its portals shall not be, 'Here pleasure is the chief good,' but 'This is an arena for character.' He who leaves this garden shall not owe to it the yearning for happiness and comfort, but an immovably steadfast moral discipline. Your children, like yourself, were born in the East, which loves what is monstrous, superhuman, exaggerated. If you entrust them to me, they must learn to govern themselves. At the helm stands moral earnestness, which, however, does not exclude the joyous cheerfulness natural to our people; the sails will be trimmed by moderation, the noblest quality of the Greek nation."

"I understand," Cleopatra interrupted, with drooping head. "Interwoven with the means of securing the children's welfare, you set before the mother's eyes the qualities she has lacked. I know that long ago you abandoned the teachings of Epicurus and the Stoa, and with an earnest aim before your eyes sought your own paths. The tempest of life swept me far away from the quiet garden where we sought the purest delight. Now I have learned to know the perils which threaten those who see the chief good in happiness. It stands too high for mortals, for in the changeful stir of life it remains unattainable, and yet it is too low an aim for their struggles, for there are worthier objects. Yet one saying of Epicurus we both believed, and it has always stood us in good stead: 'Wisdom can obtain no more precious contribution to the happiness of mortal life than the possession of friendship.'"

She held out her hand as she spoke, and while, deeply agitated, he raised it to his lips, she went on: "You know I am on the eve of the last desperate battle—if the gods will—shoulder to shoulder with Antony. Therefore I shall not be permitted to watch your work of education; yet I will aid it. When the children question you about their mother, you will be obliged to restrain yourself from saying: 'Instead of striving for the painless peace of mind, the noble pleasure of Epicurus, which once seemed to her the highest good, she constantly pursued fleeting amusements. The Oriental recklessly squandered her once noble gifts of intellect and the wealth of her people, yielded to the hasty impulses of her passionate nature.' But you shall also say to them: 'Your mother's heart was full of ardent love, she scorned what was base, strove for the highest goal, and when she fell, preferred death to treachery and disgrace.'"

Here she paused, for she thought she heard footsteps approaching, and then exclaimed anxiously: "I am waiting—expecting. Perhaps Antony cannot escape from the paralyzing grasp of despair. To fight the last battle without him, and yet under the gaze of his wrathful, gloomy eyes, once so full of sunshine, would be the greatest sorrow of my life. Archibius, I may confess this to you, the friend who saw love for this man develop in the breast of the child—— But what does this mean? An uproar! Have the people rebelled? Yesterday the representatives of the priesthood, the members of the museum, and the leaders of the army assured me of their changeless fidelity and love. Dion belonged to the Macedonian men of the Council; yet I have already declared, in accordance with the truth, that I never intended to persecute him on Cæsarion's account. I do not even know—and do not desire to know—the refuge of the lately wedded pair. Or has the new tax levied, the command to seize the treasures of the temple, driven them to extremities? What am I to do? We need gold to bid the foe defiance, to preserve the independence of the throne, the country, and the people. Or have tidings from Rome——? It is becoming serious—and the noise is growing louder."

"Let me see what they want," Archibius anxiously interrupted, hastening to the door; but just at that moment the Introducer opened it, crying, "Mark Antony is approaching the Lochias, attended by half Alexandria!"

"The noble Imperator is returning!" fell from the bearded lips of the commander of the guard, ere the courtier's words had died away; and even while he spoke Iras pressed past him, shrieking as if half frantic: "He is coming! He is here! I knew he would come! How they are shouting and cheering! Out with you, men! If you are willing, my royal mistress, we will greet him from the balcony of Berenike. If we only had——"

"The twins—little Alexander!" interrupted Cleopatra, with blanched face and faltering voice. "Put on their festal garments."

"Quick—the children, Zoe!" cried Iras, completing the order and clapping her hands. Then she turned to the Queen with the entreaty: "Be calm, my royal mistress, be calm, I beseech you. We have ample time. Here is the vulture crown of Isis, and here the other. Antony's slave, Eros, has just come in, panting for breath. The Imperator, he says, will appear as the new Dionysus. It would certainly please his master—though he had not commissioned him to request it—if you greeted him as the new Isis.—Help me, Hathor. Nephoris, tell the usher to see that the fan-bearers and the other attendants, women and men, are in their places.—Here are the pearl and diamond necklaces for your throat and bosom. Take care of the robe. The transparent bombyx is as delicate as a cobweb, and if you tear it—— No, you must not refuse. We all know how it pleases him to see his goddess in divine majesty and beauty."

Cleopatra, with glowing cheeks and throbbing heart, made no further objection to donning the superb festal robe, strewn with glimmering pearls and glittering gems. It would have been more in harmony with her feelings to meet the returning Antony in the plain, dark garb which, since her arrival at home, she had exchanged for a richer one only on festal occasions; but Antony was coming as the new Dionysus, and Eros knew what would please his master.

Eight nimble hands, which were often aided by

Iras's skilful fingers, toiled busily, and soon the latter could hold up the mirror before Cleopatra, exclaiming from the very depths of her heart, "Like the foam-born Aphrodite and the golden Hathor!"

Then Iras, who, in adorning her beloved mistress, had forgotten love, hate, and envy, and amid her eager haste barely found time for a brief, fervent prayer for a happy issue of this meeting, threw the broad folding-doors as wide as if she were about to reveal to the worshippers in the temple the image of the god in the innermost sanctuary.

A long, echoing shout of surprise and delight greeted the Queen, for the courtiers, hastily summoned, were already awaiting her without, from the grey-haired epistolograph to the youngest page. Regally attired women in her service raised the floating train of her cloak; others, in sacerdotal robes, were testing the ease of movement of the rings on the sistrum rods, men and boys were forming into lines according to the rank of each individual, and the chief fan-bearer gave the signal for departure. After a short walk through several halls and corridors, the train reached the first court-yard of the palace, and there ascended the few steps leading to the broad platform at the entrance-gate which overlooked the whole Bruchium and the Street of the King, down which the expected hero would approach.

The distant uproar of the multitude had sounded threatening, but now, amid the deafening din, they could distinguish every shout of welcome, every joyous greeting, every expression of delight, surprise, applause, admiration, and homage, known to the Greek and Egyptian tongues.

Only the centre and end of the procession were visible. The head had reached the Corner of the Muses, where, concealed by the old trees in the garden, it moved on between the Temple of Isis and the land owned by Didymus. The end still extended to the Choma, whence it had started.

All Alexandria seemed to have joined it.

Men large and small, of high and low degree, old and young, the lame and the crippled, mingled with the throng, sweeping onward among horses and carriages, carts and beasts of burden, like a mountain torrent dashing wildly down to the valley. Here a loud shriek rang from an overturned litter, whose bearers had fallen. Yonder a child thrown to the ground screamed shrilly, there a dog trodden under the feet of the crowd howled piteously. So clear and resonant were the shouts of joy that they rose high above the flutes and tambourines, the cymbals and lutes of the musicians, who followed the man approaching in the robes of a god.

The head of the procession now passed beyond the Corner of the Muses and came within view of the platform.

There could be no doubt to whom this ovation was given, for the returning hero was in the van, high above all the other figures. From the golden throne borne on the shoulders of twelve black slaves he waved his long thyrsus in greeting to the exulting multitude. Before the bacchanalian train which accompanied him, and behind the musicians who followed, moved two elephants bearing between them, as a light burden, some unrecognizable object covered with a purple cloth. Now the column had passed between the pylons through the lofty gateway which separated the palace from the Street of the King, and stopped opposite to the platform.

While officials, Scythians, and body-guards of all shades of complexion, on foot and on horseback, kept back the throng by force where friendly warning did not avail, Cleopatra saw her lover descend from the throne and give a signal to the Indian slave who guided the elephants. The cloth was flung aside, revealing to the astonished eyes of the spectators a bouquet of flowers such as no Alexandrian had ever beheld. It consisted entirely of blossoming rose-bushes. The red flowers formed a circle in the centre, surrounded by a broad light garland of white ones. The whole gigantic work rested like an egg in its cup in a holder of palm fronds which, as it were, framed it in graceful curving outlines. More than a thousand blossoms were united in this peerless bouquet, and the singular gigantic gift was characteristic of its giver.

He advanced on foot to the platform, his figure towering above the brown, light-hued, and black freedmen and slaves who followed as, on the monuments of the Pharaohs, the image of the sovereign dominates those of the subjects and foes.

He could look down upon the tallest men, and the width of his shoulders was as remarkable as his colossal height. A long, gold-broidered purple mantle, floating to his ancles, increased his apparent stature. Powerful arms, with the swelling muscles of an athlete, were extended from his sleeveless robe towards the beloved Queen.

The well-formed head, thick dark hair, and magnificent beard corresponded with the powerful figure. Formerly these locks had adorned the head of the youth with the blue-black hue of the raven's plumage; now the threads of grey scattered abundantly through them were concealed by the aid of dye. A thick wreath of vine leaves rested on the Imperator's brow, and leafy vine branches, to which clung several dark bunches of grapes, fell over his broad shoulders and down his back, which was covered like a cloak, not by a leopard-skin, but that of a royal Indian tiger of great size—he had slain it himself in the arena. The head and paws of the animal were gold, the eyes two magnificent sparkling sapphires. The clasp of the chain, by which the skin was suspended, as well as that of the gold belt which circled the Imperator's body above the hips, was covered with rubies and emeralds. The wide armlets above his elbows, the ornaments on his broad breast, nay, even his red morocco boots, glittered and flashed with gems.

Radiant as his former fortunes seemed the magnificent attire of this mighty fallen hero, who but yesterday had shrunk timidly and sadly from the eyes of his fellow-men. His features, too, were large, noble, and beautiful in outline; but, though his pale cheeks were adorned with the borrowed crimson of youth, half a century of the maddest pursuit of pleasure and the torturing excitement of the last few weeks had left traces only too visible; for the skin hung in loose bags beneath the large eyes; wrinkles furrowed his brow and radiated in slanting lines from the corners of his eyes across his temples.

Yet not one of those whom this bedizened man of fifty was approaching thought of seeing in him an aged, bedecked dandy; it was an instinct of his nature to surround himself with pomp and splendour and, moreover, his whole appearance was so instinct with power that scorn and mockery shrank abashed before it.

How frank, gracious, and kindly was this man's face, how sincere the heart-felt emotion which sparkled in his eyes, still glowing with the fire of youth, at the sight of the woman from whom he had been so long parted! Every feature beamed with the most ardent tenderness for the royal wife whom he was approaching, and the expression on the lips of the giant varied so swiftly from humble, sorrowful anguish of mind to gratitude and delight, that even the hearts of his foes were touched. But when, pressing his hand on his broad breast, he advanced towards the Queen, bending so low that it seemed as if he would fain kiss her feet, when in fact the colossal figure did sink kneeling before her, and the powerful arms were outstretched with fervent devotion like a child beseeching help, the woman who had loved him throughout her whole life with all the ardour of her passionate soul was overpowered by the feeling that everything which stood between them, all their mutual offences, had vanished. He saw the sunny smile that brightened her beloved, ever-beautiful face, and then—then his own name reached his ears from the lips to which he owed the greatest bliss love had ever offered. At last, as if intoxicated by the tones of her voice, which seemed to him more musical than the songs of the Muses; half smiling at the jest which, even in the most serious earnest, he could not abandon; half moved to the depths of his soul by the power of his newly awakening happiness after such sore sorrow, he pointed to the gigantic bouquet, which three slaves had lifted down from the elephant and were bearing to the Queen. Cleopatra, too, was overwhelmed with emotion.

This floral gift imitated, on an immense scale, the little bouquet which the famous young general had taken from her father's hand before the gate of the garden of Epicurus to present to her as his first gift. That had also been composed of red roses, surrounded by white ones. Instead of palm fronds, it had been encircled only by fern leaves. This was one of the beautiful offerings which Antony's gracious nature so well understood how to choose. The bouquet was a symbol of the unprecedented generosity natural to this large-minded man. No magic goblet had compelled him to approach her thus and with such homage. Nothing had constrained him, save his overflowing heart, his constant, fadeless love.

As if restored to youth, transported by some magic spell to the happy days of early girlhood, she forgot her royal dignity and the hundreds of eyes which rested upon him as if spell-bound; and, obedient to an irresistible impulse of the heart, she sank upon the broad, heaving breast of the kneeling hero. Laughing joyously in the clear, silvery tones which are usually heard only in youth, he clasped her in his strong arms, raised her slender figure in its floating royal mantle from the ground, kissed her lips and eyes, held her aloft in the soaring attitude of the Goddess of Victory, as if to display his happiness to the eyes of all, and at last placed her carefully on her feet again like some treasured jewel.

Then, turning to the children, who were waiting at their mother's side, he lifted first little Alexander, then the twins, to kiss them; and, while holding Helios and Selene in his arms, as if the joy of seeing them again had banished their weight, the shouts which had arisen when the Queen sank on his breast again burst forth.

The ancient walls of the Lochias palace had never heard such acclamations. They passed from lip to lip, from hundreds to hundreds and, though those more distant did not know the cause, they joined in the shouts. Along the whole vast stretch from the Lochias to the Choma the cheers rang out like a single, heart-stirring, inseparable cry, echoing across the harbour, the ships lying at anchor, the towering masts, to the cliff amid the sea where Barine was nursing her new-made husband.

CHAPTER XX.

THE property of the freedman Pyrrhus was a flat rock in the northern part of the harbour, scarcely larger than the garden of Didymus at the Corner of the Muses, a desolate spot where neither tree nor blade of grass grew. It was called the Serpent Island, though the inhabitants had long since rid it of these dangerous guests, which lived in great numbers in the neighbouring cliffs. Not even the poorest crops would grow in soil so hostile to life, and those who chose it for a home were compelled to bring even the drinking-water from the continent.

This desert, around which hovered gulls, sea-swallows, and sea-eagles, had been for several weeks the abode of the fugitives, Dion and Barine. They still occupied the two rooms which had been assigned to them on their arrival. During the day the sun beat fiercely down upon the yellow chalky rock. There was no shade save in the house and at the foot of a towering cliff in the southern part of the island, the fishermen's watch-tower.

There were no works of human hands save a

little Temple of Poseidon, an altar of Isis, the large house owned by Pyrrhus, solidly constructed by Alexandrian masons, and a smaller one for the freedman's married sons and their families. A long wooden frame, on which nets were strung to dry, rose on the shore. Near it, towards the north, in the open sea, was the anchorage of the larger sea-going ships and the various skiffs and boats of the fisher folk. Dionikos, Pyrrhus's youngest son, who was still unmarried, built new boats and repaired the old ones.

His two strong, taciturn brothers, with their wives and children, his father Pyrrhus, his wife and their youngest child, a daughter, Dione, a few dogs, cats, and chickens, composed the population of the Serpent Island.

Such were the surroundings of the newly wedded pair, who had been reared in the capital. At first many things were strange to them, but they accommodated themselves to circumstances with a good grace, and both had admitted to each other, long before, that life had never been so equable and peaceful.

During the first week Dion's wound and fever still harassed him, but the prediction of Pyrrhus that the pure, fresh sea-air would benefit the sufferer had been fulfilled, and the monotonous days had passed swiftly enough to the young bride in caring for the invalid.

The wife of Pyrrhus—"mother," as they all

called her—had proved to be a skilful nurse, and her daughters-in-law and young Dione were faithful and nimble assistants. During the time of anxiety and nursing, Barine had formed a warm friendship for them. If the taciturn men avoided using a single unnecessary word, the women were all the more ready to gossip; and it was a pleasure to talk to pretty Dione, who had grown up on the island and was eager to hear about the outside world.

Dion had long since left his couch and the house, and each day looked happier, more content with himself and his surroundings. At first his feverish visions had shown him his dead mother, pointing anxiously at his new-made wife, as if to warn him against her. During his convalescence he remembered them and they conjured up the doubt whether Barine could endure the solitude of this desolate cliff, whether she would not lose the bright serenity of soul whose charm constantly increased. Would it be any marvel if she should pine with longing in this solitude, and even suffer physically from their severe privations?

The perception that love now supplied the place of all which she had lost pleased him, but he forbade himself to expect that this condition of affairs could be lasting. Nothing save exaggerated self-conceit would induce the hope. But he must have undervalued his own power of attraction—or Barine's love—for with each passing week the cheerful serenity of her disposition gained fresh steadfastness and charm. He, too, had the same experience; it was long since he had felt so vigorous, untrammelled, and free from care. His sole regret was the impossibility of sharing the political life of the city at this critical period; and at times he felt some little anxiety concerning the fate and management of his property, though, even if his estates were confiscated, he would still retain a competence which he had left in the hands of a trustworthy money-changer. Barine shared everything that concerned him, even these moods, and this led him to tell her about the affairs of the city and the state, in which she had formerly taken little interest, his property in Alexandria and the provinces. With what glad appreciation she listened, when she went out with him from the northern anchorage on the open sea, or sat during long winter evenings making nets, an art which she had learned from Dione!

Her lute had been sent to her from the city, and what pleasure her singing afforded her husband and herself; how joyously their hosts, old and young, listened to the melody!

A few book-rolls had also come, and Dion enjoyed discussing their contents with Barine. He himself read very little, for he was rarely indoors during the day. The fourth week after his arrival he was able to aid, with arms whose muscles had been steeled in the palæstra, the men in their fishing, and Dionikos in his boat-building.

The close, constant, uninterrupted companionship of the married pair revealed to each unexpected treasures in the other, which, perhaps, might have remained forever concealed in city life. Here each was everything to the other, and this undisturbed mutual life soon inspired that blissful consciousness of inseparable union which usually appears only after years, as the fairest fruit of a marriage founded on love.

Doubtless there were hours when Barine longed to see her mother and others who were dear to her, but the letters which arrived from time to time prevented this yearning from becoming a source of actual pain.

Prudence required them to restrict their intercourse with the city. But, whenever Pyrrhus went to market, letters reached the island delivered at the fish auction in the harbour by Anukis, Charmian's Nubian maid, to the old freedman, who had become her close friend.

So the time came when Dion could say without self-deception that Barine was content in this solitude, and that his love and companionship supplied the place of the exciting, changeful life of the capital. Though letters came from her mother, sister, or Charmian, her grandfather, Gorgias, or Archibius, not one transformed the wish to leave her desolate hiding-place into actual homesickness, but each brought fresh subjects for conversation, and among them many which, by arousing the interest of both, united them more firmly.

The second month of their flight a letter arrived from Archibius, in which he informed them that they might soon form plans for their return, for Alexas, the Syrian, had proved a malicious traitor. He had not performed the commission entrusted to him of winning Herod to Antony's cause, but treacherously deserted his patron and remained with the King of the Jews. When, with unprecedented shamelessness, he sought Octavianus to sell the secrets of his Egyptian benefactor, he was arrested and executed in his own home, Laodicea.

Now, their friend continued, Cleopatra's eyes as well as her husband's were opened to the true character of Barine's most virulent accuser. The influence of Philostratus, too, was of course destroyed by his brother's infamous deed. Yet they must wait a little longer; for Cæsarion had joined the Ephebi, and Antyllus had been invested with the *toga virilis*. They could now undertake many things independently, and Cæsarion often made remarks which showed that he would not cease to lay plots for Barine.

Dion feared nothing from the royal boy on his own account, but for his wife's sake he dared not disregard his friend's warning. This was hard; for though he still felt happy on the island, he longed to install the woman he loved in his own house, and every impulse of his nature urged him to be present at the meetings of the Council in these fateful times. Therefore he was more than ready to risk returning to the city, but Barine entreated him so earnestly not to exchange the secure happiness they enjoyed here for a greater one, behind which might lurk the heaviest misfortune, that he yielded. Another letter from Charmian soon proved the absolute necessity of continuing to exercise caution.

Even from the island they could perceive that everything known as festal pleasure was rife in Alexandria, and bore along in its mad revelry the court and the citizens. When the wind blew from the south, it brought single notes of inspiring music or indistinct sounds of the wildest popular rejoicing.

The fisherman's daughter, Dione, often called them to the strand to admire the galleys adorned with fabulous splendour, garlanded with flowers, and echoing with the music of lutes and the melody of songs. Sails of purple embroidered silk bore the vessels over the smooth tide. Once the watchers even distinguished, upon a barge richly adorned with gilded carving, young female slaves who, with floating hair and transparent sea-green robes, handled, in the guise of Nereids, light sandal-wood oars with golden blades. Often the breeze bore to the island the perfumes which surrounded the galleys, and on calm nights the magnificent ships, surrounded by the magical illumination of many-hued lamps, swept across the mirror-like surface of the waves. Among the voyagers were gods, goddesses, and heroes who, standing or reclining in beautiful groups, represented scenes from the myths and history. On the deck of the Queen's superb vessel guests crowned with wreaths lay on purple couches, under garlands of flowers, eating choice viands and draining golden wine-cups.

On other nights the illumination of the shore of the Bruchium rendered it as bright as day. The huge dome of the Serapeum on the Rhakotis, covered with lamps, towered above the flat roofs of the city like the starry firmament of a smaller world which had descended to earth. Every temple and palace was transformed into a giant candelabrum, and the rows of lamps on the quay stretched like tendrils of light from the dazzlingly illuminated marble Temple of Poseidon to the palace at Lochias, steeped in radiance.

When Pyrrhus or one of his sons returned from market they described the festivals and shows, banquets, races, and endless pleasure excursions arranged by the court, which made the citizens fairly hold their breath. It was a prosperous time for the fishermen; the Queen's cooks took all their wares and paid a liberal price.

January had come, when another letter arrived from Charmian. Dion and Barine had watched in vain for any unusual events on Cleopatra's birthday, but on Antony's, a few days later, there was plenty of music and shouting, and in the evening an unusually magnificent illumination.

Two days after, this letter was delivered to Pyrrhus by his dusky friend Anukis.

Her inquiry whether he thought it prudent to convey visitors to his guests was answered in the negative, for since Octavianus had been in Asia, the harbour swarmed with the boats of spies, and a single act of imprudence might bring ruin.

Charmian's letter, too, was even better calculated to curb Dion's increasing desire to return home than the fisherman's warning.

True, the beginning contained good news of Barine's relatives, and then informed Dion that his uncle, the Keeper of the Seal, was fairly revelling in bliss. His inventive gifts were taxed more than ever. Every day brought a festival, every night magnificent banquets. One spectacle, excursion, or hunting party followed another. In the theatres, the Odeum, the Hippodrome, no more brilliant performances, races, naval battles, gladiatorial struggles, and combats between beasts had been given, even before Actium. Dion himself had formerly attended the entertainments of those who belonged to the court circle, the society of "Inimitable Livers." It had been revived again, but Antony called them the "Comrades of Death."

This was significant. Every one knows that the end is drawing near, and imitates the Pharaoh to whom the oracle promised six years of life, and who convicted it of falsehood and made them twelve by carousing during the night also.

The Queen's meeting with her husband, which she had previously reported, had been magnificent. "At that time," she wrote, "we hoped that a more noble life would begin, and Mark Antony, awakened and elevated by his rekindled love, would regain his former heroic power; but we were mistaken; Cleopatra, it is true, toiled unceasingly, but her lover with his enormous bunch of roses gave the signal for the maddest revelry which the imagination of the wildest devotee of pleasure could conceive. The performances of the Inimitable Livers were far surpassed by those of the "Comrades of Death."

"Antony is at their head, and he, whose giant frame resists even the most unprecedented demands, succeeds in stupefying himself and forgetting the impending ruin. When he comes to us after a night of revelry his eyes sparkle as brightly, his deep voice has as clear a ring, as at the beginning of the banquet. The Queen is his goddess; and who could remain unmoved when the giant bows obediently to the nod of his delicate sovereign, and devises and offers the most unprecedented things to win a smile from her lips? The changeful, impetuous wooing of youth lies far behind him, but his homage, which the Ephebi of to-day would perhaps term antiquated, has always seemed to me as if a mountain were bending before a star. The stranger who sees her in his company believes her a happy woman. Amid the fabulous radiance of the festal array, when all who surround her admire, worship, and strew flowers in her path, one might believe that the old sunny days had returned; but when we are alone, how rarely I see her smile! Then she plans for the tomb which, under Gorgias's direction, is rapidly rising, and considers with him the best method of rendering it an inaccessible place of retreat.

"She decided everything, down to the carving on the stone sarcophagi. In addition, there are to be rooms and chambers in the lower story for the reception of her treasures. Beneath them she has had corridors made for the pitch and straw which, if the worst should come, are to be lighted. She will then give to the flames the gold and silver, gems and jewels, ebony and ivory, the costly spices—in short, all her valuables. The pearls alone are worth many kingdoms. Who can blame her if she prefers to destroy them rather than leave them for the foe?

"The garden in which you grew up, Barine, is now the scene of the happy, busy life led by Alexander and the twins. There, under my brother's guidance, they frolic, build, and dig. Cleopatra goes to it whenever she longs for repose after the pursuit of pleasures which have lost their zest.

"When, the day before yesterday, Antony, crowned with ivy as the new Dionysus, drove up the Street of the King in the golden chariot drawn by tamed lions, to bring her, the new Isis, from the Lochias in a lotus flower made of silver and white paste, drawn by four snow-white steeds, she pointed to the glittering train and said: 'Between the quiet of the philosopher's garden, where I began my life and still feel most at ease, and the grave, where nothing disturbs my last repose, stretches the Street of the King, with this deafening tumult, this empty splendour. It is mine.'

"O child, it was very different in former days! She loved Mark Antony with passionate ardour. He was the first man in the world, and yet he bowed before the supremacy of her will. The longing of the awakening heart, the burning ambition which already kindled the soul of the child, had alike found satisfaction, and the world beheld how the mortal woman, Cleopatra, for her lover and herself, could steep this meagre life with the joys of the immortals. He was grateful for them, and the most generous of men laid at the feet of the 'Great Queen of the East' the might of Rome and the kings of two quarters of the globe.

"These years were spent by both in one long revel. His marriage with Octavia brought the first awakening. It was hard and painful. He had not deserted Cleopatra for a woman's sake, but on account of his endangered power and sovereignty. But the unloved Octavia constrained him to look up to her with respectful admiration—nay, she became dear to him.

"A fierce battle for him and his heart arose between the two. It was fought with very different weapons, and Cleopatra conquered. The revel, the dream began again. Then came Actium, the disenchantment, the awakening, the fall, the flight from the world. Our object was not to let him relapse into intoxication, to rouse the hero's strength and courage from their slumber, render him for love's sake a fellow-combatant in the common cause.

"But he had become accustomed to see in her the giver of ecstasy. The only thing that he still desired was to drain the cup of pleasure in her society till all was over. She sees this, grieves over it, and leaves no means of rousing him to fresh energy untried; yet how rarely he rallies his powers to earnest labour!

"While she is fortifying the mouths of the Nile and the frontiers of the country, building ship after ship, arming and negotiating, she can not resist him when he summons her to new pleasures.

"Though so many of the traits which rendered him great and noble have vanished, she can not give up the old love and clings steadfastly to him because, because—I know not why. A woman's loving heart does not question motives and laws. Besides, he is the father of her children and, in playing with them, he regains the old joyousness of mood so enthralling to the heart.

"Since Archibius has taken charge of them, they can dispense with Euphronion, their tutor. The clever man knows Rome, Octavianus, and those who surround him, so he was chosen as an envoy. His object was to induce the conqueror to transfer the sovereignty of Egypt to the boys Antonius Helios, and Alexander, but Cæsar vouchsafed no answer to the mediator in Antony's affairs —nay, did not even grant him an audience.

"To Cleopatra Octavianus promised friendly treatment, and the fulfilment of her wish concerning the boys if—and now came the repetition of the old demand—she would put Antony out of the world or deliver him into his hands.

"This demand, which contains base treachery, was impossible for her noble soul. Since she had resolved to build the tomb, granting it became impossible, yet Octavianus made every effort to tempt her to the base deed. True, the death of this one man would have spared much bloodshed. The Cæsar knows how to choose his tools. He sent here as negotiator a clever young man, who possessed great charms of mind and person. No plan to prejudice the Queen against her husband and persuade her to commit the treachery was left untried. He went so far as to assure Cleopatra that in former years she had won the Cæsar's heart, and that he still loved her. She accepted these assurances at their true value and remained steadfast.

"Antony at first paid no heed to the intriguer. But when he learned what means he employed, and especially how he made use of the surrender of one of Cæsar's murderers, which he himself had long regretted, to brand him as an ungrateful traitor, he would not have been Mark Antony if he had accepted it quietly. He was completely his old self when he ordered the smooth fellow—who, however, had come as the ambassador of the mighty victor—to be scourged, sent him back to Rome, and wrote a letter to Octavianus, in which he complained of the man's arrogance and presumption, adding—spite of my heavy heart I can not help smiling when I think of it—that misfortune had rendered him unusually irritable; yet if his action perhaps displeased Cæsar, he might treat his freedman Hipparchus, who was in his power, as he had served Thyrsus!

"You see that his gay arrogance has not deserted him. Trouble slips away from him as rain is shaken from the coarse military cloak which he wore in the Parthian war, and therefore it cannot exert its purifying power.

"When we consider that, a few years ago, this man, as it were, doubled himself when peril was most threatening, his conduct now, on the eve of the decisive struggle, is intelligible only to those who know him as we do. If he fights, he will no longer do so to save himself, or even to conquer, but to die an honourable death. If he still enjoys the pleasures offered, he believes that he can thus mitigate for himself the burden of defeat, and diminish the grandeur of the conqueror's victory. In the eyes of the world, at least, a man who can still revel like Antony is only half vanquished. Yet the lofty tone of his mind was lowered. The surrender of the murderer of Cæsar—his name was Turullius—proves it.

"And this, Barine—tell your husband so—this is what fills me with anxiety and compels me to entreat you not to think of returning home yet.

"Antony is now the jovial companion of his son, and permits Antyllus to share all his own pleasures. Of course, he heard of Cæsarion's passion, and is disposed to help the poor fellow. He has often said that nothing would better serve to rouse the dreamer from torpor than your charming vivacity. As the earth could scarcely have swallowed you up, you would be found; he, too, should be glad to hear you sing again. I know that search will be made for you.

"How imperiously this state of affairs requires you to exercise caution needs no explanation. On the other hand, you may find comfort in the tidings that Cleopatra intends to send Cæsarion with his tutor Rhodon to Ethiopia, by way of the island of Philæ. Archibius heard through Timagenes that Octavianus considers the son of Cæsar, whose face so wonderfully resembles his father's, a dangerous person, and this opinion is the boy's death-warrant. Antyllus, too, is going on a journey. His destination is Asia, where he is to seek to propitiate Octavianus and make him new offers. As you know, he was betrothed to his daughter Julia. The Queen ceased long ago to believe in the possibility of victory, yet, spite of all the demands of the "Comrades of Death" and her own cares, she toils unweariedly in preparing for the defence of the country. She is doubtless the only member of that society who thinks seriously of the approaching end.

"Now that the tomb is rising, she ponders constantly upon death. She, who was taught by Epicurus to strive for freedom from pain and is so sensitive to the slightest bodily suffering, is still seeking a path which, with the least agony, will lead to the eternal rest for which she longs. Iras and the younger pupils of Olympus are aiding her. The old man furnishes all sorts of poisons, which she tries upon various animals—nay, recently even on criminals sentenced to death. All these experiments seem to prove that the bite of the uræus serpent, whose image on the Egyptian crown symbolizes the sovereign's instant power over life and death, stills the heart most swiftly and with the least suffering.

"How terrible these things are! What pain it causes to see the being one loves most, the mother of the fairest children, so cruelly heighten the anguish of parting, choose death, as it were, for a constant companion, amid the whirl of the gayest amusements! She daily looks all his terrors in the face, yet with proud contempt turns her back upon the bridge which might perhaps enable her for a time to escape the monster. This is grand, worthy of her, and never have I loved her more tenderly.

"You, too, must think of her kindly. She deserves it. A noble heart which sees itself forced to pity a foe, easily forgives; and was she ever your enemy?

"I have written a long, long letter to solace your seclusion from the world and relieve my own heart. Have patience a little while longer. The time is not far distant when Fate itself will release you from exile. How often your relatives, Archibius and Gorgias, whom I now see frequently in the presence of the Queen, long to visit you!—but they, too, believe that it might prove a source of danger."

The warnings in this letter were confirmed by another from Archibius, and soon after they heard that Cæsarion had really sailed up the Nile for Ethiopia with his tutor Rhodon, and Antyllus had been sent to Asia to visit Octavianus. The latter had received him, it is true; but sent him home without making any pledges.

These tidings were not brought by letter, but by Gorgias himself, whose visit surprised them one evening late in March.

Rarely had a guest received a more joyous welcome. When he entered the bare room, Barine was making a net and telling the fisherman's daughter Dione the story of the wanderings of Ulysses. Dion, too, listened attentively, now and then correcting or explaining her descriptions, while carving a head of Poseidon for the prow of a newly built boat.

As Gorgias unexpectedly crossed the threshold, the dim light of the lamp fed by kiki-oil seemed transformed into sunshine. How brightly their eyes sparkled, how joyous were their exclamations of welcome and surprise! Then came questions, answers, news! Gorgias was obliged to share the family supper, which had only waited the return of the father who had brought the guest.

The fresh oysters, langustæ, and other dishes served tasted more delicious to the denizen of the city than the most delicious banquets of the "Comrades of Death" to which he was now frequently invited by the Queen.

All that Pyrrhus said voluntarily and told his sons in reply to their questions was so sensible and related to matters which, because they were new to Gorgias, seemed so fascinating that, when Dion's good wine was served, he declared that if Pyrrhus would receive him he, too, would search for pursuers and be banished here.

When the three again sat alone before the plain clay mixing vessel it seemed to the lonely young couple as if the best part of the city life which they had left behind had found its way to them, and what did they not have to say to one another! Dion and Barine talked of their hermit life, Gorgias of the Queen and the tomb, which was at the same time a treasure chamber. The slanting walls were built as firmly as if they were intended to last for centuries and defy a violent assault. The centre of the lower story was formed by a lofty hall of vast dimensions, in whose midst were the large marble sarcophagi. Men were working busily upon the figures in relief intended for the decoration of the sides and lids. This hall, whose low arched ceiling was supported by three pairs of heavy columns, was furnished like a reception-room. The couches, candelabra, and altars were already being made. Charmian had kept the fugitives well informed. In the subterranean chambers at the side of the hall, and in the second story, which could not be commenced until the ceiling was completed, store-rooms were to be made, and below and beside them were passages for ventilation and the storage of combustible materials.

Gorgias regretted that he could not show his friend the hall, which was perhaps the handsomest and most costly he had ever created. The noblest material—brown porphyry, emerald-green serpentine, and the dark varieties of marble—had been used, and the mosaic and brass doors, which were nearing completion, were masterpieces of Alexandrian art. To have all this destroyed was a terrible thought, but even more unbearable was that of its object—to receive the body of the Queen.

Again rapturous admiration of this greatest and noblest of women led Gorgias to enthusiastic rhapsodies, until Dion exercised his office of soberer, and Barine asked tidings of her mother, her grandparents, and her sister. There was nothing but good news to be told. True, the architect had to wage a daily battle with the old philosopher, who termed it an abuse of hospitality to remain so long at his friend's with his whole family; but thus far Gorgias had won the victory, even against Berenike, who wished to take her father and his household to her own home.

Cleopatra had purchased the house and garden of Didymus at thrice their value, the architect added. He was now a wealthy man, and had commissioned him to build a new mansion. The land facing the sea and near the museum had been found, but the handsome residence would not be completed until summer. The dry Egyptian air would have permitted him to roof it sooner, but there were many of Helena's wishes—most of them very sensible ones—to be executed.

Barine and Dion glanced significantly at each other; but the architect, perceiving it, exclaimed: "Your mute language is intelligible enough, and I confess that for five months Helena has seemed to me the most attractive of maidens. I see, too, that she has some regard for me. But as soon as I stand before *her*—the Queen, I mean—and hear her voice, it seems as if a tempest swept away every thought of Helena, and it is not in my nature to deceive any one. How can I woo a girl whom I so deeply honour—your sister, Barine—when the image of another rules my soul?"

Dion reminded him of his own words that the Queen was loved only as a goddess and, without waiting for his reply, turned the conversation to other topics.

It was three hours after midnight when Pyrrhus warned Gorgias that it was time for departure. When the fisherman's fleetest boat was at last bearing him back to the city he wondered whether girls who, before marriage, lived like Helena in undisturbed seclusion, would really be better wives and more content with every lot than the much-courted Barine, whom Dion had led from the gayest whirl of life in the capital to the most desolate solitude.

This delightful evening was followed by a day of excitement and grave anxiety. It had been necessary to conceal the young couple from the collector's officials, who took from Pyrrhus part of his last year's savings, and the large new boat which he used to go out on the open sea. The preparations for war required large sums; all vessels suitable for the purpose were seized for the fleet, and all residents of the city and country shared the same fate as Pyrrhus.

Even the temple treasures were confiscated, and yet no one could help saying to himself that the vast sums which, through these pitiless extortions, flowed into the treasury, were used for the pleasures of the court as well as for the equipment of the fleet and the army.

Yet so great was the people's love for the Queen, so high their regard for the independence of Egypt, so bitter their hate of Rome, that there was no rebellion.

How earnestly Cleopatra, amid all the extravagant revels, from which she could not too frequently absent herself, toiled to advance the military preparations, could be seen even by the exiles from their cliff; for work in two dock-yards was continued day and night, and the harbour was filled with vessels. Ships of war were continually moving to and fro, and from the Serpent Island they witnessed constantly, often by starlight, the drilling of the oarsmen and of whole squadrons upon the open sea. Sometimes a magnificent state galley appeared, on whose deck was Antony, who inspected the hastily equipped fleet to make the newly recruited sailors one of those kindling speeches in which he was a master hard to surpass. Two sons of Pyrrhus were now numbered in the crews of the recently built war ships. They had been impressed into the service in April, and though Dion had placed a large sum at their father's disposal to secure their release, the attempt was unsuccessful.

So there had been sorrow and tears in the contented little colony of human beings on the lonely cliff, and when Dionysus and Dionichos had a day's leave of absence to visit their relatives, they complained of the cruel haste with which the young men were drilled and wearied to exhaustion, and spoke of the sons of citizens and peasants who had been dragged from their villages, their parents, and their business to be trained for seamen. There was great indignation among them, and they listened only too readily to the agitators who whispered how much better they would have fared on the galleys of Octavianus.

Pyrrhus entreated his sons not to join any attempt at mutiny; the women, on the contrary, would have approved anything which promised to release the youths from their severe service, and their bright cheerfulness was transformed into anxious depression. Barine, too, was no longer the same. She had lost her joyous activity, her eyes were often wet with tears, and she moved with drooping head as if some heavy care oppressed her.

Was it the heat of April, with its desert winds, which had brought the transformation? Had longing for the changeful, exciting life of former days at last overpowered her? Was solitude becoming unendurable? Was her husband's love no longer sufficient to replace the many pleasures she had sacrificed?—No! It could not be that; never had she gazed with more devoted tenderness into Dion's face than when entirely alone with him in shady nooks. She who in such hours looked the very embodiment of happiness and contentment, certainly was neither ill nor sorrowful.

Dion, on the contrary, held his head high early and late, and appeared as proud and self-conscious as though life was showing him its fairest face. Yet he had heard that his estates had been sequestrated, and that he owed it solely to the influence of Archibius and his uncle, that his property, like that of so many others, had not been added to the royal treasures. But what disaster could he not have speedily vanquished in these days?

A great joy—the greatest which the immortals can bestow upon human beings—was dawning for him and his young wife, and in May the women on the island shared her blissful hope.

Pyrrhus brought from the city an altar and a marble statue of Ilythyia, the Goddess of Birth, called by the Romans Lucina, which his friend Anukis had given him, in Charmian's name, for the young wife. She had again spoken of the serpents which lived in such numbers in the neighbouring islands, and her question whether it would be difficult to capture one alive was answered by the freedman in the negative.

The image of the goddess and the altar were erected beside the other sanctuaries, and how often the stone was anointed by Barine and the women of the fisherman's family!

Dion vowed to the goddess a beautiful temple on the cliff and in the city if she would be gracious to his beloved young wife.

When, in June, the noonday sun blazed most fiercely, the fisherman brought to the cliff Helena, Barine's sister, and Chloris, Dion's nurse, who had been a faithful assistant of his mother, and afterwards managed the female slaves of the household.

How joyously and gratefully Barine held out her arms to her sister! Her mother had been prevented from coming only by the warning that her disappearance would surely attract the attention of the spies. And the latter were very alert; for Mark Antony had not yet given up the pursuit of the singer, nor had the attorney Philostratus recalled the proclamation offering two talents for the capture of Dion, and both the latter's palace and Berenike's house were constantly watched.

It seemed more difficult for the quiet Helena to accommodate herself to this solitude than for her gayer-natured sister. Plainly as she showed her love for Barine, she often lapsed into reverie, and every evening she went to the southern side of the cliff and gazed towards the city, where her grandparents doubtless sorely missed her, spite of the careful attention bestowed upon them in Gorgias's house.

Eight days had passed since her arrival, and life in this wilderness seemed more distasteful than on the first and the second; the longing for her grandparents, too, appeared to increase; for that day she had gone to the shore, even under the burning rays of the noonday sun, to gaze towards the city.

How dearly she loved the old people!

But Dion's conjecture that the tears sparkling in Helena's eyes when she entered their room at dusk were connected with another resident of the capital, spite of his wife's indignant denial, appeared to be correct; for, a short time after, clear voices were heard in front of the house, and when a deep, hearty laugh rang out, Dion started up, exclaiming, "Gorgias never laughs in that way, except when he has had some unusual piece of good fortune!"

He hurried out as he spoke, and gazed around; but, notwithstanding the bright moonlight, he could see nothing except Father Pyrrhus on his way back to the anchorage.

But Dion's ears were keen, and he fancied he heard subdued voices on the other side of the dwelling. He followed the sound without delay and, when he turned the corner of the building, stopped short in astonishment, exclaiming as a low cry rose close before him:

"Good-evening, Gorgias! I'll see you later. I won't interrupt you."

A few rapid steps took him back to Barine, and as he whispered, "I saw Helena out in the moonlight, soothing her longing for her grandparents in Gorgias's arms," she clapped her hands and said, smiling:

"That's the way one loses good manners in this solitude. To disturb the first meeting of a pair of lovers! But Gorgias treated us in the same way in Alexandria, so he is now paid in his own coin."

The architect soon entered the room, with Helena leaning on his arm. Hour by hour he had missed her more and more painfully, and on the eighth day found it impossible to endure life's burden longer without her. He now protested that he could approach her mother and grandparents as a suitor with a clear conscience; for on the third day after Helena's departure the relation between him and the Queen had changed. In Cleopatra's presence the image of the granddaughter of Didymus became even more vivid than that of the peerless sovereign had formerly been in Helena's. Outside of the pages of poetry he had never experienced longing like that which had tortured him during the past few days.

CHAPTER XXI.

THIS time the architect could spend only a few hours on the Serpent Island, for affairs in the city were beginning to wear a very serious aspect, and the building of the monument was pushed forward even during the night. The interior of the first story was nearly completed and the rough portion of the second was progressing. The mosaic workers, who were making the floor of the great hall, had surpassed themselves. It was impossible to wait longer for the sculptures which were to adorn the walls. At present slabs of polished black marble were to occupy the places intended for bronze reliefs; the utmost haste was necessary.

Octavianus had already reached Pelusium; even if Seleukus, the commander of the garrison, held the strong fortress a long time, a part of the hostile army might appear before Alexandria the following week.

A considerable force, however, was ready to meet him. The fleet seemed equal to that of the enemy; the horsemen whom Antony had led before the Queen would delight the eye of any one versed in military affairs; and the Imperator hoped much from the veterans who had served under him in former times, learned to know his generosity and open hand in the hour of prosperity, and probably had scarcely forgotten the eventful days when he had cheerfully and gaily shared their perils and privations.

Helena remained on the cliff, and her longing for the old couple had materially diminished. Her hands moved nimbly, and her cheerful glance showed that the lonely life on the island was beginning to unfold its charms to her.

The young husband, however, had grown very uneasy. He concealed it before the women, but old Pyrrhus often had much difficulty in preventing his making a trip to the city which might imperil, on the eve of the final decision, the result of their long endurance and privation. Dion had often wished to set sail with his wife for a great city in Syria or Greece, but fresh and mighty obstacles had deterred him. A special danger lay in the fact that every large vessel was thoroughly searched before it left the harbour, and it was impossible to escape from it without passing through the narrow straits east of the Pharos or the opening in the Heptastadium, both of which were easily guarded. The calm moderation that usually distinguished the young counsellor had been transformed into feverish restlessness, and the heart of his faithful old monitor had also lost its poise; for an encounter between the fleet in which his sons served and that of Octavianus was speedily expected.

One day he returned from the city greatly excited. Pelusium was said to have fallen.

When he ascended the cliff he found everything quiet. No one, not even Dione, came to meet him.

What had happened here?

Had the fugitives been discovered and dragged with his family to the city to be thrown into prison, perhaps sent to the stone quarries?

Deadly pale, but erect and composed, he walked towards the house. He owed to Dion and his father the greatest blessing in life, liberty, and the foundation of everything else he possessed. But if his fears were verified, if he was bereft of friends and property, even as a lonely beggar he might continue to enjoy his freedom. If, for the sake of those to whom he owed his best possession, he must surrender the rest, it was his duty to bear fate patiently.

It was still light.

Even when he had approached very near the house he heard no sound save the joyous barking of his wolf-hound, Argus, which leaped upon him.

He now laid his hand upon the lock of the door—but it was flung open from the inside.

Dion had seen him coming and, enraptured by the new happiness with which this day had blessed him, he flung himself impetuously on the breast of his faithful friend, exclaiming: "A boy, a splendid boy! We will call him Pyrrhus."

Bright tears of joy streamed down the freedman's face and fell on his grey beard; and when his wife came towards him with her finger on her lips, he whispered in a tremulous voice: "When I brought them here you were afraid that the city people would drag us into ruin, but nevertheless you received them as they deserved to be, and—he's going to name him Pyrrhus—and now!—What has a poor fellow like me done to have such great and beautiful blessings fall to my lot?"

"And I—I?" sobbed his wife. "And the child, the darling little creature!"

This day of sunny happiness was followed by others of quiet joy, of the purest pleasure, yet mingled with the deepest anxiety. They also brought many an hour in which Helena found an opportunity to show her prudence, while old Chloris and the fisherman's wife aided her by their experience.

Every one, down to the greybeard whose name the little one bore, declared that there had never been a lovelier young mother than Barine or a handsomer child than the infant Pyrrhus; but Dion could no longer endure to remain on the cliff.

A thousand things which he had hitherto deemed insignificant and allowed to pass unheeded now seemed important and imperatively in need of his personal attention. He was a father, and any negligence might be harmful to his son.

With his bronzed complexion and long hair and beard he required little aid to disguise him from his friends. In the garments shabby by long use, and with his delicate hands calloused by work in the dock-yard, any one would have taken him for a real fisherman.

Perhaps it was foolish, but the desire to show himself in the character of a father to Barine's mother and grandparents and to Gorgias seemed worth risking a slight danger; so, without informing Barine, who was now able to walk about her room, he set out for the city after sunset on the last day of July.

He knew that Octavianus was encamped in the Hippodrome east of Alexandria. The white mounds which had risen there had been recognized as tents, even from the Serpent Island. Pyrrhus had returned in the afternoon with tidings that Antony's mounted troops had defeated those of Octavianus. This time the news of victory could be trusted, for the palace at Lochias was illuminated for a festival and when Dion landed there was a great bustle on the quay. One shouted to another that all would be well. Mark Antony was his old self again. He had fought like a hero.

Many who yesterday had cursed him, to-day mingled their voices in the shouts of "Evoë!" which rang out for the new Dionysus, who had again proved his claim to godship.

The late visitor found the grandparents alone in the house of Gorgias. They had been informed of Barine's new happiness long before. Now they rejoiced with Dion, and wanted to send at once for their host and future son-in-law, who was in the city attending a meeting of the Ephebi, although he had ceased some time ago to be a member of their company. But Dion wished to greet him among the youths who had invited the architect to give them his aid in deciding the question of the course they were to pursue in the impending battle.

Yet he did not leave the old couple immediately; he was expecting two visitors—Barine's mother and Charmian's Nubian maid who, since the birth of little Pyrrhus, had come to the philosopher's every evening. The former's errand was to ask whether any news of the mother and child had been received during the day; the latter, to get the letters which she delivered the next morning at the fish-market to her friend Pyrrhus or his sons.

Anukis was the first to appear. She relieved her sympathizing heart by a brief expression of congratulations; but, gladly as she would have listened to the most minute details concerning the beloved young mother from the lips of Dion himself, she repressed her own wishes for her mistress's sake, and returned to Charmian as quickly as possible to inform her of the arrival of the unexpected guest.

Berenike bore her new dignity of grandmother with grateful joy, yet to-night she came oppressed by a grave anxiety, which was not solely due to her power of imagining gloomy events. Her brother Arius and his sons were concealed in the house of a friend, for they seemed threatened by a serious peril. Hitherto Antony had generously borne the philosopher no ill-will on the score of his intimate relations with Octavianus; but now that Octavianus was encamped outside the city, the house of the man who, during the latter's years of education, had been his mentor and counsellor, and later a greatly valued friend, was watched, by Mardion's orders, by the Scythian guard. He and his family were forbidden to enter the city, and his escape to his friend had been effected under cover of the darkness and with great danger.

The anxious woman feared the worst for her brother if Mark Antony should conquer, and yet, with her whole heart, she wished the Queen to gain the victory. She, who always feared the worst, saw in imagination the fortunes of war change—and there was reason for the belief. The bold general who had gained so many victories, and whom the defeat of Actium had only humbled, was said to have regained his former elasticity. He had dashed forward at the head of his men with the heroic courage of former days—nay, with reckless impetuosity. Rumour reported that, with the huge sword he wielded, he had dealt from his powerful charger blows as terrible as those inflicted five-and-twenty years before when, not far from the same spot, he struck Archelaus on the head. The statement that, in his golden armour, with the gold helmet framing his bearded face, he resembled his ancestor Herakles, was confirmed by Charmian, who had been borne quickly hither by a pair of the Queen's swift horses. Cleopatra might need her soon, yet she had left the Lochias to question the father about many things concerning the young mother and her boy, who was already dear to her as the first grandson of the man whose suit, it is true, she had rejected, but to whom she owed the delicious consciousness of having loved and been loved in the springtime of life.

Dion found her changed. The trying months which she had described in her letters to Barine had completely blanched her grey hair, her cheeks were sunken, and a deep line between her mouth and nose gave her pleasant face a sorrowful expression. Besides, she seemed to have been weeping and, in fact, heart-rending events had just occurred.

She had stolen away from Lochias in the midst of a revel.

Antony's victory was being celebrated. He himself presided at the banquet. Again his head and breast were wreathed with a wealth of fresh leaves and superb flowers. At his side reclined Cleopatra, robed in light-blue garments adorned with lotus-flowers which, like the little coronet on her head, glittered with sapphires and pearls. Charmian said she had rarely looked more beautiful. But she did not add that the Queen had been obliged to have rouge applied to her pale, bloodless cheeks.

It was touching to see Antony after his return from the battle, still in his suit of mail, clasp her in his arms as joyously as if he had won her back, a prize of victory, and with his vanished heroic power regained her and their mutual love. Her eyes, too, had been radiant with joy and, in the elation of her heart, she had given the horseman who, for a deed of special daring, was presented to her, a helmet and coat of mail of solid gold.

Yet, even before the revel began, she had been forced to acknowledge to herself that the commencement of the end was approaching; for, a few hours after she had so generously rewarded the man, he had deserted to the foe. Then Antony had challenged Octavianus to a duel, and received the unfeeling reply that he would find many roads to death open.

This was the language of the cold-hearted foe, secure of superior power. How sadly, too, she had been disappointed in the hope that the veterans who had served under Antony would desert their new commander at the first summons and flock to his standard!—for all her husband's efforts in this direction, spite of the bewitching power of his eloquence, failed, while every hour brought tidings of the treacherous desertion from his army of individual warriors and whole maniples. His foe deemed his cause so weak that he did not even resist Mark Antony's attempts to win the soldiers by promises.

From all these signs Cleopatra now saw plainly, in her lover's victory, only the last flicker of a dying fire; but so long as it burned he should see her follow its light.

Therefore she had entered the festal hall with the victor of the day. She had witnessed a strange festival. It began with tears and reminded Cleopatra of the saying that she herself resembled a banquet served to celebrate a victory before the battle was won. The cup-bearers had scarcely advanced to the guests with their golden vessels when Antony turned to them, exclaiming: "Pour generously, men; perhaps to-morrow you will serve another master!"

Then, unlike his usual self, he grew thoughtful and murmured under his breath, "And I shall probably be lying outside a corpse, a miserable nothing."

Loud sobs from the cup-bearers and servants followed these words; but he addressed them calmly, assuring them that he would not take them into a battle from which he expected an honourable death rather than rescue and victory.

At this Cleopatra's tears flowed also. If this reckless man of pleasure, this notorious spendthrift and disturber of the public peace, with his insatiate desires, had inspired bitter hostility, few had gained the warm love of so many hearts. One glance at his heroic figure; one memory of the days when even his foes conceded that he was never greater than in the presence of the most imminent peril, never more capable of awakening in others the hope of brighter times than amid the sorest privations; one tone of the orator's deep, resonant voice, which so often came from the heart and therefore gained hearts with such resistless power; the recollection of numberless instances of the bright cheerfulness of his nature and his boundless generosity sufficiently explained the lamentations which burst forth at that banquet, the tears which flowed—tears of genuine feeling. They were also shed for the beautiful Queen who, unmindful of the spectators, rested her noble brow, with its coronal of pearls, upon his mighty shoulder.

But the grief did not last long, for Mark Antony, shouted: "Hence with melancholy! We do not need the larva!* We know, without its aid, that

---

* At the banquets of the Egyptians a small figure in the shape of a mummy was passed around to remind the guests that they, too, would soon be in the same condition, and have no more time to enjoy life and its pleasures. The Romans imi-

pleasure will soon be over!—Xuthus, a joyous festal song!—And you, Metrodor, lead the dancers! The first beaker to the fairest, the best, the wisest, the most cherished, the most fervently beloved of women!" As he spoke he waved his goblet aloft, the flute-player, Xuthus, beckoned to the chorus, and the dancer Metrodor, in the guise of a butterfly, led forth a bevy of beautiful girls, who, in the cloud of ample robes of transparent coloured bombyx which floated around them, executed the most graceful figures and now hovered like mists, now flitted to and fro as if borne on wings, affording the most charming variety to the delighted spectators.

The "Comrades of Death" had again become companions in pleasure; and when Charmian, who did not lose sight of her mistress, noticed the sorrowful quiver of her lips and glided out of the circle of guests, the faithful Nubian had approached to inform her of Dion's arrival.

Then—but this she concealed from her friends —she hastened to her own apartments to prepare to go out, and when Iras opened the door to enter her rooms she went to speak to her about the night attendance upon the Queen. But her niece had not perceived her; shaken by convulsive sobs, she

---

tated this custom by sending the larva, a statuette in the form of a skeleton, to make the round of the revellers. The Greek love of beauty converted this ugly scarecrow into a winged genius.

had pressed her face among the cushions of a couch, and there suffered the fierce anguish which had stirred the inmost depths of her being to rave itself out with the full vehemence of her passionate nature. Charmian called her name and, weeping herself, opened her arms to her, and for the first time since her return from Actium her sister's daughter again sank upon her breast, and they held each other in a close embrace until Charmian's exclamation, "With her, for her unto death!" was answered by Iras's "To the tomb!"

This was a word which, in many an hour of the silent night, had stirred the soul of the woman who had been the youthful playmate of the Queen who, with bleeding heart, sat below among the revellers at the noisy banquet and forced her to ask the question: "Is not your fate bound to hers? What can life offer you without her?"

Now, this word was spoken by other lips, and, like an echo of Iras's exclamation, came the answer: "Unto death, like you, if she precedes us to the other world. Whatever may follow dying, nowhere shall she lack Charmian's hand and heart."

"Nor the love and service of Iras," was the answering assurance.

So they had parted, and the agitation of this fateful moment was still visible in the features of the woman who had formerly sacrificed to her royal playfellow her love, and now offered her life.

When, ere leaving Gorgias's house, she bade her friend farewell, she pressed Dion's hand with affectionate warmth and, as he accompanied her to the carriage, she informed him that, before the first encounter of the troops, Archibius had taken the royal children to his estate of Irenia, where they were at present.

"Rarely has it been my fate to experience a more sorrowful hour than when I beheld the Queen, her heart torn with anguish, bid them farewell. What fate is impending over the dear ones, who are so worthy of the greatest happiness? To see the twins and little Alexander recognized and saved from death and insult, and your boy in Barine's arms, is the last wish which I still cherish."

On returning to Lochias, Charmian had a long time to wait ere the Queen retired. She dreaded the mood in which she would leave the banquet. For months past Cleopatra had returned from the revels of the "Comrades of Death" saddened to tears, or in a blaze of indignation. How must this last banquet, which began so mournfully and continued with such reckless mirth, affect her?

At last, the second hour after midnight, Cleopatra appeared.

Charmian believed that she must be the sport of some delusion, for the Queen's eyes which, when she had left her, were full of tears, now sparkled with the radiant light of joy and, as her friend took the crown from her head, she exclaimed:

"Why did you depart from the banquet so early? Perhaps it was the last, but I remember no festival more brilliant. It was like the springtime of my love. Mark Antony would have touched the heart of a stone statue by that blending of manly daring and humble devotion which no woman can resist. As in former days, hours shrivelled into moments. We were again young, once more united. We were together here at Lochias to-night, and yet in distant years and other places. The notes of the singers, the melodies of the musicians, the figures executed by the dancers, were lost upon us. We soared back, hand in hand, to a magic world, and the fairy drama in the realms of the blessed, which passed before us in dazzling splendour and blissful joy, was the dream which I loved best when a child, and at the same time the happiest portion of the life of the Queen of Egypt.

"It began before the gate of the garden of Epicurus, and continued on the river Cydnus. I again beheld myself on the golden barge, garlanded with wreaths of flowers, reclining on the purple couch with roses strewn around me and beneath my jewelled sandals. A gentle breeze swelled the silken sails; my female companions raised their clear voices in song to the accompaniment of lutes; the perfumes floating around us were borne by the wind to the shore, conveying the tidings that the bliss believed by mortals to be reserved for the gods alone was drawing near. And even as his heart and his enraptured senses yielded to my sway, his mind, as he himself confessed, was under the thrall of mine. We both felt happy, united by ties which nothing, not even misfortune, could sever. He, the ruler of the world, was conquered, and delighted to obey the behests of the victor, because he felt that she before whom he bowed was his own obedient slave. And no magic goblet effected all this. I breathed more freely, as if relieved from the oppressive delusion—the fire had consumed it also—which had burdened my soul until a few hours ago. No magic spell, only the gifts of mind and soul which the vanquished victor, the woman Cleopatra, owed to the favour of the immortals, had compelled his lofty manhood to yield.

"From the Cydnus he brought me hither to the blissful days which we were permitted to pass in my city of Alexandria. A thousand sunny hours, musical, echoing surges which long since dashed down the stream of Time, he recalled to life, and I —I did the same, and our memories blended into one. What never-to-be-forgotten moments we experienced when, with reckless mirth, we mingled unrecognized among the joyous throng! What Olympic delight elated our hearts when the plaudits of thousands greeted us! What joys satiated our minds and senses in our own apartments! What pure, unalloyed nectar of the soul was bestowed upon us by our children—bliss which we shared with and imparted to each other until neither knew which was the giver and which the receiver! Everything sad and painful seemed to be effaced from the book of memory; and the child's dream, the fairy-tale woven by the power of imagination, stood before my soul as a reality—the same reality, I repeat, which I call my past life.

"And, Charmian, if death comes to-morrow, should I say that he appeared too early—summoned me ere he permitted life to bestow all its best gifts upon me? No, no, and again no! Whoever, in the last hour of existence, can say that the fairest dreams of childhood were surpassed by a long portion of actual life, may consider himself happy, even in the deepest need and on the verge of the grave.

"The aspiration to be first and highest among the women of her own time, which had already thrilled the young girl's heart, was fulfilled. The ardent longing for love which, even at that period, pervaded my whole being, was satisfied when I became a loving wife, mother, and Queen, and friendship, through the favour of Destiny, also bestowed upon me its greatest blessings by the hands of Archibius, Charmian, and Iras.

"Now I care not what may happen. This evening taught me that life had fulfilled its pledges. But others, too, must be enabled to remember the most brilliant of queens, who was also the most fervently beloved of women. For this I will provide: the mausoleum which Gorgias is erecting for me will stand like an indestructible wall between the Cleopatra who to-day still proudly wears the crown and her approaching humiliation and disgrace.

"Now I will go to sleep. If my awakening brings defeat, sorrow, and death, I have no reason to accuse my fate. It denied me one thing only: the painless peace which the child and the young girl recognized as the chief good; yet Cleopatra will possess that also. The domain of death, which, as the Egyptians say, loves silence, is opening its doors to me. The most absolute peace begins upon its threshold—who knows where it ends? The vision of the intellect does not extend far enough to discover the boundary where, at the end of eternity—which in truth is endless—it is replaced by something else."

While speaking, the Queen had motioned to her friend to accompany her into her chamber, from which a door led into the children's room. An irresistible impulse constrained her to open it and gaze into the dark, empty apartment.

She felt an icy chill run through her veins. Taking a light from the hand of one of the maids who attended her, she went to little Alexander's couch. Like the others, it was empty, deserted. Her head sank on her breast, the courageous calmness with which she had surveyed her whole past life failed and, like the luxuriant riot in the sky of the most brilliant hues, ere the glow of sunset suddenly yields to darkness, Cleopatra's soul, after the lofty elation of the last few hours, underwent a sudden transition and, overwhelmed by deep, sorrowful depression, she threw herself down before the twins' bed, where she lay weeping softly until Charmian, as day began to dawn, urged her to retire to rest. Cleopatra slowly rose, dried her eyes, and said: "My past life seemed to me just now like a magnificent garden, but how many serpents suddenly stretched out their flat heads with glittering eyes and forked tongues! Who tore away the flowers beneath which they lay concealed? I think, Charmian, it was a mysterious power which here, in the children's apartment, rules so strongly the most trivial as well as the strongest emotions, it was—when did I last hear that ominous word?— it was conscience. Here, in this abode of innocence and purity, whatever resembles a spot stands forth distinctly before the eyes. Here, O Charmian!—if the children were but here! If I could only—yet, no, no! It is fortunate, very fortunate that they have gone. I must be strong; and their sweet grace would rob me of my energy. But the light grows brighter and brighter. Dress me for the day. It would be easier for me to sleep in a falling house than with such a tumult in my heart."

While she was being attired in the dark robes she had ordered, loud shouts arose from the royal harbour below, blended with the blasts of the tuba and other signals directing the movements of the fleet and the army, a large body of troops having been marched during the night to the neighbouring hills overlooking the sea.

The notes sounded bold and warlike. The well-armed galleys presented a stately appearance. How often Cleopatra had seen unexpected events occur, apparent impossibilities become possible! Had not the victory of Octavianus at Actium been a miracle? What if Fate, like a capricious ruler, now changed from frowns to smiles? What if Antony proved himself the hero of yesterday, the general he had been in days of yore?

She had refused to see him again before the battle, that she might not divert his thoughts from the great task approaching. But now, as she beheld him, clad in glittering armour like the god of war himself, ride before the troops on his fiery Barbary charger, greeting them with the gay salutation whose warmth sprung from the heart and which had so often kindled the warriors to glowing enthusiasm, she was forced to do violence to her own feelings to avoid calling him and saying that her thoughts would follow his course. But she refrained, and when his purple cloak vanished from her sight her head drooped again. How different in former days were the cheers of the troops when he showed himself to them! This lukewarm response to his gay, glad greeting was no omen of victory.

CHAPTER XXII.

Dion, too, witnessed the departure of the troops. Gorgias, whom he had found among the Ephebi, accompanied him and, like the Queen, they saw, in the cautious manner with which the army greeted the general, a bad omen for the result of the battle. The architect had presented Dion to the youths as the ghost of a dead man, who, as soon as he was asked whence he came or whither he was going, would be compelled to vanish in the form of a fly. He could venture to do this; he knew the Ephebi—there was no traitor in their ranks.

Dion, the former head of the society, had been welcomed like a beloved brother risen from the dead, and he had the gratification, after so long a time, of turning the scale as speaker in a debate. True, he had encountered very little opposition, for the resolve to hold aloof from the battle against the Romans had been urged upon the Ephebi by the Queen herself through Antyllus, who, however, had already left the meeting when Dion joined it. It had seemed to Cleopatra a crime to claim the blood of the noblest sons of the city for a cause which she herself deemed lost. She knew the parents of many, and feared that Octavianus would inflict a terrible punishment upon them if, not being enrolled in the army, they fell into his power with arms in their hands.

The stars were already setting when the Ephebi accompanied their friend, singing in chorus the Hymenæus, which they had been unable to chant on his wedding day. The melody of lutes accompanied the voices, and this nocturnal music was the source of the rumour that the god Dionysus, to whom Mark Antony felt specially akin, and in whose form he had so often appeared to the people, had abandoned him amid songs and music.

The youths left Dion in front of the Temple of Isis. Gorgias alone remained with him. The architect led his friend to the Queen's mausoleum near the sanctuary, where men were toiling busily by torchlight. A light scaffolding still surrounded it, but the lofty first story, containing the real tomb, was completed, and Dion admired the art with which the exterior of the edifice suggested its purpose. Huge blocks of dark-grey granite formed the walls. The broad front—solemn, almost gloomy in aspect—rose, sloping slightly, above the massive lofty door, surmounted by a moulding bearing the winged disk of the sun. On either side were niches containing statues of Antony and

Cleopatra cast in dark bronze, and above the cornice were brazen figures of Love and Death, Fame and Silence, ennobling the Egyptian forms with exquisite works of Hellenic art.

The massive door, adorned with brass figures in relief, would have resisted a battering-ram. On the side of the steps leading to it lay Sphinxes of dark-green diorite. Everything connected with this building, dedicated to death, was grave and massive, suggesting by its indestructibility the idea of eternity.

The second story was not yet finished; masons and stone-cutters were engaged in covering the strong walls with dark serpentine and black marble. The huge windlass stood ready to raise a masterpiece of Alexandrian art. This was intended for the pediment, and represented Venus Victrix with helmet, shield, and lance, leading a band of winged gods of love, little archers at whose head Eros himself was discharging arrows, and victoriously fighting against the three-headed Cerberus, death, already bleeding from many wounds.

There was no time to see the interior of the building, for Pyrrhus expected his guest to join him at the harbour at sunrise, and the eastern sky was already brightening with the approach of dawn.

As the friends reached the landing-place the brass dome of the Serapeum, which towered above everything, was glittering with dazzling splendour.

The pennons and masts of the fleet which was about to set sail from the harbour seemed steeped in a sea of golden light. Tremulous reflections of the brazen and gilded figures on the prows of the vessels were mirrored in the undulating surface of the sea, and the long shadows of the banks of oars united galley after galley on the surface of the water like the meshes of a net.

Here the friends parted, and Dion walked down the quay alone to meet the freedman, who must have found it difficult to guide his boat out of this labyrinth of vessels. The inspection of the mausoleum had detained the young father too long and, though disguised beyond recognition, he reproached himself for having recklessly incurred a danger whose consequences—he felt this to-day for the first time—would not injure himself alone. The whole fleet was awaiting the signal for departure. The vessels which did not belong to it had been obliged to moor in front of the Temple of Poseidon, and all were strictly forbidden to leave the anchorage.

Pyrrhus's fishing-boat was in the midst, and return to the Serpent Island was impossible at present.

How vexatious! Barine was ignorant of his trip to the city, and to be compelled to leave her alone while a naval battle was in progress directly before her eyes distressed him as much as it could not fail to alarm her.

In fact, the young mother had waited from early dawn with increasing anxiety for her husband. As the sun rose higher, and the strokes of the oars propelling two hundred galleys, the shrill whistle of the flutes marking the time, the deep voices of the captains shouting orders, and the blasts of the trumpets filling the air, were heard far and near around the island, she became so overwhelmed with uneasiness that she insisted upon going to the shore, though hitherto she had not been permitted to take the air except under the awning stretched for the purpose on the shady side of the house.

In vain the women urged her not to let her fears gain the mastery and to have patience. But she would have resisted even force in order to look for him who, with her child, now comprised her world.

When, leaning on Helena's arm, she reached the shore, no boat was in sight. The sea was covered with ships of war, floating fortresses, moving onward like dragons with a thousand legs whose feet were the countless rowers arranged in three or five sets. Each of the larger galleys was surrounded by smaller ones, from most of which darted dazzling flashes of light, for they were crowded with armed men, and from the prows of the strong boarding vessels the sunbeams glittered on the large shining metal points whose office was to pierce the wooden sides of the foe. The gilded statues in the prows of the large galleys shone and sparkled in the broad radiance of the day-star, and flashes of light also came from the low hills on the shore. Here Mark Antony's soldiers were stationed, and the sunbeams reflected from the helmets, coats of mail, and lance-heads of the infantry, and the armour of the horsemen quivered with dazzling brilliancy in the hot air of the first day of an Egyptian August.

Amid this blazing, flashing, and sparkling in the morning air, so steeped in warmth and radiance, the sounds of warlike preparations from the land and fleet constantly grew louder. Barine, exhausted, had just sunk into a chair which Dione, the fisherman's daughter, had placed in the shade of the highest rock on the northwestern shore of the flat island, when a crashing blast of the tuba suddenly echoed from all the galleys in the Egyptian fleet, and the whole array of vessels filed past the Pharos at the opening of the harbour into the open sea.

There the narrow ranks of the wooden giants separated and moved onward in broader lines. This was done quietly and in the same faultless order as a few days before, when a similar manœuvre had been executed under the eyes of Mark Antony.

The longing for combat seemed to urge them steadily forward.

The hostile fleet, lying motionless, awaited the

attack. But the Egyptian assailants had advanced majestically only a few ships' lengths towards the Roman foe when another signal rent the air. The women whose ears caught the waves of sound said afterwards that it seemed like a cry of agony—it had given the signal for a deed of unequalled treachery. The slaves, criminals, and the basest of the mercenaries on the rowers' benches in the hold had doubtless long listened intently for it, and, when it finally came, the men on the upper benches raised their long oars and held them aloft, which stopped the work of those below, and every galley paused, pointing at the next with the wooden oars outstretched like fingers, as if seized with horror. The celerity and faultless order with which the raising of the oars was executed and vessel after vessel brought to a stand would have been a credit to an honourable captain, but the manœuvre introduced one of the basest acts ever recorded in history; and the women, who had witnessed many a *naumachia* and understood its meaning, exclaimed as if with a single voice: "Treachery! They are going over to the enemy!"

Mark Antony's fleet, created for him by Cleopatra, surrendered, down to the last galley, to Cæsar's heir, the victor of Actium; and the man to whom the sailors had vowed allegiance, who had drilled them, and only yesterday had urged them to offer a gallant resistance, saw from one of the downs on the shore the strong weapons on which he had based the fairest hopes, not shattered, but delivered into the hands of the enemy!

The surrender of the fleet to the foe—he knew it—sealed his destruction; and the women on the shore of the Serpent Island, who were so closely connected with those on whom this misfortune fell, suspected the same thing. The hearts of both were stirred, and their eyes grew dim with tears of indignation and sorrow. They were Alexandrians, and did not desire to be ruled by Rome.

Cleopatra, daughter of the Macedonian house of the Ptolemies, had the sole right to govern the city of her ancestors, founded by the great Macedonian. The sorrow they had themselves endured through her sank into insignificance beside the tremendous blow of Fate which in this hour reached the Queen.

The Roman and Egyptian fleet returned to the harbour as one vast squadron under the same commander, and anchored in the roadstead of the city, which was now its precious booty.

Barine had seen enough, and returned to the house with drooping head. Her heart was heavy, and her anxiety for the man she loved hourly increased.

It seemed as if the very day-star shrank from illuminating so infamous a deed with friendly light; for the dazzling, searching sun of the first of August veiled its radiant face with a greyish-white mist, and the desecrated sea wrinkled its brow, changed its pure azure robe to yellowish grey and blackish green, while the white foam hissed on the crests of the angry waves.

As twilight began to approach, the anxiety of the deserted wife became unendurable. Not only Helena's wise words of caution, but the sight of her child, failed to exert their usual influence; and Barine had already summoned the son of Pyrrhus to persuade him to take her in his boat to the city, when Dione saw a boat approaching the Serpent Island from the direction of the sea.

A short time after, Dion sprang on shore and kissed from his young wife's lips the reproaches with which she greeted him.

He had heard of the treachery of the fleet while entering a hired boat with the freedman in the harbour of Eunostus, Pyrrhus's having been detained with the other craft before the Temple of Poseidon.

The experienced pilot had been obliged to steer the boat in a wider curve against the wind through the open sea, and was delayed a long time by a number of the war vessels of the fleet.

Danger and separation were now passed, and they rejoiced in the happiness of meeting, yet could not feel genuine joy. Their souls were oppressed by anxiety concerning the fate of the Queen and their native city.

As night closed in the dogs barked violently,

and they heard loud voices on the shore. Dion, with a presentiment that misfortune was threatening himself and his dear ones, obeyed the summons.

No star illumined the darkness. Only the wavering light of a lantern on the strand and another on the nearest island illumined the immediate vicinity, while southward the lights in the city shone as brightly as ever.

Pyrrhus and his youngest son were just pushing a boat into the water to release from the sands another which had run aground in a shallow near the neighbouring island.

Dion sprang in with them, and soon recognized in the hail the voice of the architect Gorgias.

The young father shouted a joyous greeting to his friend, but there was no reply.

Soon after, Pyrrhus landed his belated guest on the shore. He had escaped—as the fisherman explained—a great danger; for had he gone to the other island, which swarmed with venomous serpents, he might easily have fallen a victim to the bite of one of the reptiles.

Gorgias grasped Dion's hand but, in reply to his gay invitation to accompany him to the house at once, he begged him to listen to his story before joining the ladies.

Dion was startled. He knew his friend. When his deep voice had such a tone of gloomy discouragement, and his head drooped so mournfully, some terrible event had befallen him.

His foreboding had been correct. The first tidings pierced his own soul deeply.

He was not surprised to learn that the Romans ruled Alexandria; but a small band of the conquerors, who had been ordered to conduct themselves as if they were in a friendly country, had forced their way into the architect's large house to occupy the quarters assigned to them. The deaf grandmother of Helena and Barine, who had but half comprehended what threatened the citizens, terrified by the noisy entrance of the soldiers, had had another attack of apoplexy, and closed her eyes in death before Gorgias set out for the island.

But it was not only this sad event, which must grieve the hearts of the two sisters, that had brought the architect in a stranger's boat to the Serpent Island at so late an hour. His soul was so agitated by the horrible incidents of the day that he needed to seek consolation among those from whom he was sure to find sympathy.

Nor was it wholly the terrible things Fate had compelled him to witness which induced him to venture out upon the sea so recklessly, but still more the desire to bring to the fugitives the happy news that they might return with safety to their native city.

Deeply agitated—nay, confused and overpowered by all he had seen and experienced—the architect, usually so clear and, with all his mental vivacity, so circumspect, began his story. A remonstrance from Dion induced him to collect his thoughts and describe events in the order in which they had befallen him.

CHAPTER XXIII.

AFTER accompanying Dion to the harbour, the architect had gone to the Forum to converse with the men he met there, and learn what they feared and expected in regard to the future fate of the city.

All news reached this meeting-place first, and he found a large number of Macedonian citizens who, like himself, wished to discuss passing events in these decisive hours.

The scene was very animated, for the most contradictory messages were constantly arriving from the fleet and the army.

At first they were very favourable; then came the news of the treason, and soon after of the desertion of the cavalry and foot soldiers.

A distinguished citizen had seen Mark Antony, accompanied by several friends, dashing down the quay. The goal of their flight was the little palace on the Choma.

Grave men, whose opinion met with little opposition, thought that it was the duty of the Imperator—now that Fate had decided against him, and nothing remained save a life sullied by disgrace—to put himself to death with his own hand, like Brutus and so many other noble Romans. Tidings soon came that he had attempted to do what the best citizens expected.

Gorgias could not endure to remain longer in the Forum, but hastened to the Choma, though it was difficult to force his way to the wall, where a breach had been made. He had found the portion of the shore from which the promontory ran densely crowded with people—from whom he learned that Antony was no longer in the palace—and the sea filled with boats.

A corpse was just being borne out of the little palace on the Street of the King and, among those who followed, Gorgias recognized one of Antony's slaves. The man's eyes were red with weeping. He readily obeyed the architect's sign and, sobbing bitterly, told him that the hapless general, after his army had betrayed him, fled hither. When he heard in the palace that Cleopatra had preceded him to Hades, he ordered his body-slave Eros to put an end to his life also. The worthy man drew back, pierced his own breast with his sword, and sank dying at his master's feet; but Antony, exclaiming that Eros's example had taught him his duty, thrust the short sword into his breast with his own hand. Yet deep and severe as was the wound, it did not destroy the tremendous vitality of the gigantic Roman. With touching entreaties he implored the bystanders to kill him, but no one could bring himself to commit the deed. Meanwhile Cleopatra's name, coupled with the wish to follow her, was constantly on the lips of the Imperator.

At last Diomedes, the Queen's private secretary, appeared, to bring him, by her orders, to the mausoleum where she had taken refuge.

Antony, as if animated with fresh vigour, assented, and while being carried thither gave orders that Eros should have a worthy burial. Even though dying, it would have been impossible for the most generous of masters to permit any kindness rendered to pass unrequited.

The slave again wept aloud as he uttered the words, but Gorgias hastened at once to the tomb.

The nearest way, the Street of the King, had become so crowded with people who had been forced back by Roman soldiers, between the Theatre of Dionysus and the Corner of the Muses, that he had been compelled to reach the building through a side street.

The quay was already unrecognizable, and even in the other streets the populace showed a foreign aspect. Instead of peaceful citizens, Roman soldiers in full armour were met everywhere. Instead of Greek, Egyptian, and Syrian faces, fair and dark visages of alien appearance were seen.

The city seemed transformed into a camp. Here he met a cohort of fair-haired Germans;

yonder another with locks of red whose home he did not know; and again a *vexil* of Numidian or Pannonian horsemen.

At the Temple of the Dioscuri he was stopped. A Hispanian maniple had just seized Antony's son Antyllus and, after a hasty court-martial, killed him. His tutor, Theodotus, had betrayed him to the Romans, but the infamous fellow was being led with bound hands after the corpse of the hapless youth, because he was caught in the act of hiding in his girdle a costly jewel which he had taken from his neck. Before his departure for the island Gorgias heard that the scoundrel had been sentenced to crucifixion.

At last he succeeded in forcing a passage to the tomb, which he found surrounded on all sides by Roman lictors and the Scythian guards of the city, who, however, permitted him, as the architect, to pass.

The numerous obstacles by which he had been delayed spared him from becoming an eye-witness of the most terrible scenes of the tragedy which had just ended; but he received a minute description from the Queen's private secretary, a well-disposed Macedonian, who had accompanied the wounded Antony, and with whom Gorgias had become intimately acquainted during the building of the mausoleum.

Cleopatra had fled to the tomb as soon as the fortune of war turned in favour of Octavianus. No one was permitted to accompany her except Charmian and Iras, who had helped her close the heavy brazen door of the massive building. The false report of her death, which had induced Antony to put an end to his life, had perhaps arisen from the fact that the Queen was literally in the tomb.

When, borne in the arms of his faithful servants, he reached the mausoleum, mortally wounded, the Queen and her attendants vainly endeavoured to open the heavy brazen portal. But Cleopatra ardently longed to see her dying lover. She wished to have him near to render the last services, assure him once more of her devotion, close his eyes, and, if it was so ordered, die with him.

So she and her attendants had searched the place, and when Iras spoke of the windlass which stood on the scaffold to raise the heavy brass plate bearing the bas-relief of Love conquering Death, the Queen and her friends hastened up the stairs, the bearer below fastened the wounded man to the rope, and Cleopatra herself stood at the windlass to raise him, aided by her faithful companions.

Diomedes averred that he had never beheld a more piteous spectacle than the gigantic man hovering between heaven and earth in the agonies of death and, while suffering the most terrible torture, extending his arms longingly towards the woman he loved. Though scarcely able to speak, he tenderly called her name, but she made no reply; like Iras and Charmian, she was exerting her whole strength at the windlass in the most passionate effort to raise him. The rope running over the pulley cut her tender hands; her beautiful face was terribly distorted; but she did not pause until they had succeeded in lifting the burden of the dying man higher and higher till he reached the floor of the scaffolding. The frantic exertion by which the three women had succeeded in accomplishing an act far beyond their strength, though it was doubled by the power of the most earnest will and ardent longing, would nevertheless have failed in attaining its object had not Diomedes, at the last moment, come to their assistance. He was a strong man, and by his aid the dying Roman was seized, drawn upon the scaffolding, and carried down the staircase to the tomb in the first story.

When the wounded general had been laid on one of the couches with which the great hall was already furnished, the private secretary retired, but remained on the staircase, an unnoticed spectator, in order to be at hand in case the Queen again needed his assistance. Flushed from the terrible exertion which she had just made, with tangled, dishevelled locks, gasping and moaning, Cleopatra, as if out of her senses, tore open her robe, beat her breast, and lacerated it with her nails. Then, pressing her own beautiful face on her lover's wound to stanch the flowing blood, she lavished upon him all the endearing names which she had bestowed on the dying man in the springtime of their love.

His terrible suffering made her forget her own and the sad fate impending. Tears of pity fell like the refreshing drops of a shower upon the still unwithered blossoms of their love, and brought those which, during the preceding night, had revived anew, to their last magnificent unfolding.

Boundless, limitless as her former passion for this man, was now the grief with which his agonizing death filled her heart.

All that Mark Antony had been to her in the heyday of life, all their mutual experiences, all that each had received from the other, had returned to her memory in clear and vivid hues during the banquet which had closed a few hours ago. Now these scenes, condensed into a narrow compass, again passed before her mental vision, but only to reveal more distinctly the depth of misery of this hour. At last anguish forced even the clearest memories into oblivion: she saw nothing save the tortures of her lover; her brain, still active, revealed solely the gulf at her feet, and the tomb which yawned not only for Antony, but for herself.

Unable to think of the happiness enjoyed in the past or to hope for it in the future, she gave herself up to uncontrolled despair, and no woman of the people could have yielded more absolutely to the consuming grief which rent her heart, or expressed it in wilder, more frantic language, than did this great Queen, this woman who as a child had been so sensitive to the slightest suffering, and whose after-life had certainly not taught her to bear sorrow with patience. After Charmian, at the dying man's request, had given him some wine, he found strength to speak coherently, instead of moaning and sighing.

He tenderly urged Cleopatra to secure her own safety, if it could be done without dishonour, and mentioned Proculejus as the man most worthy of her confidence among the friends of Octavianus. Then he entreated her not to mourn for him, but to consider him happy; for he had enjoyed the richest favours of Fortune. He owed his brightest hours to her love; but he had also been the first and most powerful man on earth. Now he was dying in the arms of Love, honourable as a Roman who succumbed to Romans.

In this conviction he died after a short struggle.

Cleopatra had watched his last breath, closed his eyes, and then thrown herself tearlessly on her lover's body. At last she fainted, and lay unconscious with her head upon his marble breast.

The private secretary had witnessed all this, and then returned with tearful eyes to the second story. There he met Gorgias, who had climbed the scaffolding, and told him what he had seen and heard from the stairs. But his story was scarcely ended when a carriage stopped at the Corner of the Muses and an aristocratic Roman alighted.

This was the very Proculejus whom the dying Antony had recommended to the woman he loved as worthy of her confidence.

"In fact," Gorgias continued, "he seemed in form and features one of the noblest of his haughty race. He came commissioned by Octavianus, and is said to be warmly devoted to the Cæsar, and a well-disposed man. We have also heard him mentioned as a poet and a brother-in-law of Mæcenas. A wealthy aristocrat, he is a generous patron of literature, and also holds art and science in high esteem. Timagenes lauds his culture and noble nature. Perhaps the historian was right; but where the object in question is the state and its advantage, what we here regard as worthy of a free man appears to be considered of little moment at the court of Octavianus. The lord to whom he gives his services intrusted him with a difficult task, and Proculejus doubtless considered it his duty to make every effort to perform it—and yet—— If I see aright, a day will come when he will curse this, and the obedience with which he, a free man, aided Cæsar—— But listen.

"Erect and haughty in his splendid suit of armour, he knocked at the door of the tomb. Cleopatra had regained consciousness and asked— she must have known him in Rome—what he desired.

"He had come, he answered courteously, by the command of Octavianus, to negotiate with her, and the Queen expressed her willingness to listen, but refused to admit him into the mausoleum.

"So they talked with each other through the door. With dignified composure, she asked to have the sons whom she had given to Antony—not Cæsarion—acknowledged as Kings of Egypt.

"Proculejus instantly promised to convey her wishes to Cæsar, and gave hopes of their fulfilment.

"While she was speaking of the children and their claims—she did not mention her own future—the Roman questioned her about Mark Antony's death, and then described the destruction of the dead man's army and other matters of trivial importance. Proculejus did not look like a babbler, but I felt a suspicion that he was intentionally trying to hold the attention of the Queen. This proved to be his design; he had been merely waiting for Cornelius Gallus, the commander of the fleet, of whom you have heard. He, too, ranks among the chief men in Rome, and yet he made himself the accomplice of Proculejus.

"The latter retired as soon as he had presented the new-comer to the hapless woman.

"I remained at my post and now heard Gallus assure Cleopatra of his master's sympathy. With the most bombastic exaggeration he described how bitterly Octavianus mourned in Mark Antony the friend, the brother-in-law, the co-ruler and sharer in so many important enterprises. He had shed burning tears over the tidings of his death. Never had more sincere ones coursed down any man's cheeks.

"Gallus, too, seemed to me to be intentionally prolonging the conversation.

"Then, while I was listening intently to understand Cleopatra's brief replies, my foreman, who, when the workmen were driven away by the Romans, had concealed himself between two blocks of granite, came to me and said that Proculejus had just climbed a ladder to the scaffold in the rear of the monument. Two servants followed, and they had all stolen down into the hall.

"I hastily started up. I had been lying on the floor with my head outstretched to listen.

"Cost what it might, the Queen must be warned. Treachery was certainly at work here.

"But I came too late.

"O Dion! If I had only been informed a few minutes before, perhaps something still more terrible might have happened, but the Queen would have been spared what now threatens her. What can she expect from the conqueror who, in order to seize her alive, condescends to outwit a noble, defenceless woman, who has succumbed to superior power?

"Death would have released the unhappy Queen from sore trouble and horrible shame. And she had already raised the dagger against her life. Before my eyes she flung aloft her beautiful arm with the flashing steel, which glittered in the light of the candles in the many-branched candelabra beside the sarcophagi. But I will try to remain calm! You shall hear what happened in regular order. My thoughts grow confused as the terrible scene recurs to my memory. To describe it as I saw it, I should need to be a poet, an artist in words; for what passed before me happened on a stage—you know, it was a tomb. The walls were of dark stone—dark, too, were the pillars and ceiling—all dark and glittering; most portions were smoothly polished stone, shining like a mirror. Near the sarcophagi, and around the candelabra as far as the vicinity of the door, where the rascally trick was played, the light was brilliant as in a festal hall. Every blood-stain on the hand, every scratch, every wound which the desperate woman had torn with her own nails on her bosom, which gleamed snow-white from her black robes, was distinctly visible. Farther away, on the right and left, the light was dim, and near the side walls the darkness was as intense as in a real tomb. On the smooth porphyry columns, the glittering black marble and serpentine—here, there, and everywhere —flickered the wavering reflection of the candle-light. The draught kept it continually in motion, and it wavered to and fro in the hall, like the restless souls of the damned. Wherever the eye turned it met darkness. The end of the hall seemed black—black as the anteroom of Hades—yet through it pierced a brilliant moving bar; sunbeams which streamed from the stairway into the tomb and amid which danced tiny motes. How the scene impressed the eye! The home of gloomy Hecate! And the Queen and her impending fate! A picture flooded with light, standing forth in radiant relief against the darkness of the heavy, majestic forms surrounding it in a wide circle. This tomb in this light would be a palace meet for the gloomy rule of the king of the troop of demons conjured up by the power of a magician—if they have a ruler. But where am I wandering? 'The artist!' I hear you exclaim again, 'the artist! Instead of rushing forward and interposing, he stands studying the light and its effects in the royal tomb.' Yes, yes; I had come too late, too late—far too late! On the stairs leading to the lower story of the building I saw it, but I was not to blame for the delay—not in the least!

"At first I had been unable to see the men—or even a shadow; but I beheld plainly in the brightest glare of the light the body of Mark Antony on the couch and, in the dusk farther towards the right, Iras and Charmian trying to raise a trapdoor. It was the one which closed the passage leading to the combustible materials stored in the cellar. A sign from the Queen had commanded them to fire it. The first steps of the staircase, down which I was hastening, were already behind me—then—then Proculejus, with two men, suddenly dashed from the intense darkness on the other side. Scarcely able to control myself, I sprang down the remaining steps, and while Iras's shrill cry, 'Poor Cleopatra, they will capture you!' still rang in my ears, I saw the betrayed Queen turn from the door through which, resolved on death, she was saying something to Gallus, perceive Proculejus close behind her, thrust her hand into her girdle, and with the speed of lightning—you have already heard so—throw up her arm with the little dagger to bury the sharp blade in her breast. What a picture! In the full radiance of the brilliant light, she resembled a statue of triumphant victory or of noble pride in great deeds accomplished; and then, then, only an instant later, what an outrage was inflicted!

"Like a robber, an assassin, Proculejus rushed upon her, seized her arm, and wrested the weapon from her grasp. His tall figure concealed her from me. But when, struggling to escape from the ruffian's clutch, she again turned her face towards the hall, what a transformation had occurred! Her eyes—you know how large they are—were twice their usual size, and blazed with scorn, fury, and hatred for the traitor. The cheering light had become a consuming fire. So I imagine the vengeance, the curse which calls down ruin upon the head of a foe. And Proculejus, the great lord, the poet whose noble nature is praised by the authors on the banks of the Tiber, held the defenceless woman, the worthy daughter of a brilliant line of kings, in a firm grasp, as if it required the exertion of all his strength to master this delicate embodiment of charming womanhood. True, the proud blood of the outwitted lioness urged her to resist this profanation, and Proculejus—an enviable honour—made her feel the superior strength of his arm. I am no prophet, but Dion, I repeat, this shameful struggle and the glances which flashed upon him will be remembered to his dying hour. Had they been darted at me, I should have cursed my life. They blanched even the Roman's cheeks. He was lividly pale as he completed what he deemed his duty. His own aristocratic hands were degraded to the menial task of searching the garments of a woman, the Queen, for forbidden wares, poisons or weapons. He was aided by one of Cæsar's freedmen, Epaphroditus, who is said to stand so high in the favour of Octavianus.

"The scoundrel also searched Iras and Charmian, yet all the time both Romans constantly spoke in cajoling terms of Cæsar's favour, and his desire to grant Cleopatra everything which was due a Queen.

"At last she was taken back to Lochias, but I felt like a madman; for the image of the unfortunate woman pursued me like my shadow. It was no longer a vision of the bewitching sovereign—

nay, it resembled the incarnation of despair, tearless anguish, wrath demanding vengeance. I will not describe it; but those eyes, those flashing, threatening eyes, and the tangled hair on which Antony's blood had flowed—terrible, horrible! My heart grew chill, as if I had seen upon Athene's shield the head of the Medusa with its serpent locks.

"It had been impossible for me to warn her in time, or even to seize the traitor's arm—I have already said so—and yet, yet her shining image gazed reproachfully at me for my cowardly delay. Her glance still haunts me, robbing me of calmness and peace. Not until I gaze into Helena's pure, calm eyes will that terrible vision of the face, flooded by light in the midst of the tomb, cease to haunt me."

His friend laid his hand on his arm, spoke soothingly to him, and reminded him of the blessings which this terrible day—he had said so himself—had brought.

Dion was right to give this warning; for Gorgias's bearing and the very tone of his voice changed as he eagerly declared that the frightful events had been followed by more than happy ones for the city, his friend, and Barine.

Then, with a sigh of relief, he continued: "I pursued my way home like a drunken man. Every attempt to approach the Queen or her attendants was baffled, but I learned from Charmian's clever

Nubian that Cleopatra had been permitted, in Cæsar's name, to choose the palace she desired to occupy, and had selected the one at Lochias.

"I did not make much progress towards my house; the crowd in front of the great gymnasium stopped me. Octavianus had gone into the city, and the people, I heard, had greeted him with acclamations and flung themselves on their knees before him. Our stiff-necked Alexandrians in the dust before the victor! It enraged me, but my resentment was diminished.

"The members of the gymnasium all knew me. They made way and, ere I was aware of it, I had passed through the door. Tall Phryxus had drawn my arm through his. He appears and vanishes at will, is as alert as he is rich, sees and hears everything, and manages to secure the best places. This time he had again succeeded; for when he released me we were standing opposite to a newly erected tribune.

"They were waiting for Octavianus, who was still in the hypostyle of Euergetes receiving the homage of the epitrop, the members of the Council, the gymnasiarch, and I know not how many others.

"Phryxus said that on Cæsar's entry he had held out his hand to his former tutor, bade him accompany him, and commanded that his sons should be presented. The philosopher had been distinguished above every one else, and this will benefit you and yours; for he is Berenike's brother, and therefore your wife's uncle. What he desires is sure to be granted. You will hear at once how studiously the Cæsar distinguishes him. I do not grudge it to the man; he interceded boldly for Barine; he is lauded as an able scholar, and he does not lack courage. In spite of Actium and the only disgraceful deed with which, to my knowledge, Mark Antony could be reproached—I mean the surrender of Turullius—Arius remained here, though the Imperator might have held the friend of Julius Cæsar's nephew as a hostage as easily as he gave up the Emperor's assassin.

"Since Octavianus encamped before the city, your uncle has been in serious danger, and his sons shared his peril. Surely you must know the handsome, vigorous young Ephebi.

"We were not obliged to wait long in the gymnasium ere the Cæsar appeared on the platform; and now—if your hand clenches, it is only what I expect—now all fell on their knees. Our turbulent, rebellious rabble raised their hands like pleading beggars, and grave, dignified men followed their example. Whoever saw me and Phryxus will number us among the kneeling lickspittles; for had we remained standing we should certainly have been dragged down. So we followed the example of the others."

"And Octavianus?" asked Dion eagerly.

"A man of regal bearing and youthful aspect; a beardless face of the finest chiselling, a profile as beautiful as if created for the coin-maker; all the lines sharp and yet pleasing; every inch an aristocrat; but the very mirror of a cold nature, incapable of any lofty aspiration, any warm emotion, any tenderness of feeling. All in all, a handsome, haughty, calculating man, whose friendship would hardly benefit the heart, but from whose enmity may the immortals guard all we love!'

"Again he led Arius by the hand. The philosopher's sons followed the pair. When he stood on the stage, looking down upon the thousands kneeling before him, not a muscle of his noble face—it is certainly that—betrayed the slightest emotion. He gazed at us like a farmer surveying his flocks and, after a long silence, said curtly in excellent Greek that he absolved the Alexandrians from all guilt towards him: first—he counted as if he were summoning individual veterans to reward them—from respect for the illustrious founder of our city, Alexander, the conqueror of the world; secondly, because the greatness and beauty of Alexandria filled him with admiration; and, thirdly—he turned to Arius as he spoke—to give pleasure to his admirable and beloved friend.

"Then shouts of joy burst forth.

"Every one, from the humblest to the greatest, had had a heavy burden removed from his mind, and the throng had scarcely left the gymnasium when they were again laughing saucily enough, and there was no lack of biting and innocent jests.

The fat carpenter, Memnon—who furnished the wood-work for your palace—exclaimed close beside me that formerly a dolphin had saved Arius from the pirates; now Arius was saving marine Alexandria from the robbers. So the sport went on. Philostratus, Barine's first husband, offered the best butt for jests. The agitator had good reason to fear the worst; and now, clad in black mourning robes, ran after Arius, whom but a few months ago he persecuted with the most vindictive hatred, continually repeating this shallow bit of verse:

"'If he is a wise man, let the wise aid the wise.'

"Reaching home was not easy. The street was swarming with Roman soldiers. They fared well enough; for in the joy of their hearts many a prosperous citizen who saw his property saved invited individual warriors, or even a whole maniple, to the taverns or cook-shops, and the stock of wine in Alexandrian cellars will be considerably diminished to-night.

"Many, as I have already said, had been quartered in the houses, with orders to spare the property of the citizens; and it was in this way that the misfortune with which I commenced my narrative befell the grandmother. She died before my departure.

"All the gates of the city will now stand open to you, and the niece of Arius and her husband will be received with ovations. I don't grudge

Barine the good fortune; for the way in which your noble wife, who had cast her spell over me too, flung aside what is always dear to the admired city beauty and found on the loneliest of islands a new world in love, is worthy of all admiration and praise. For yourself, I dread new happiness and honours; if they are added to those which Fate bestowed upon you in such a wife and your son Pyrrhus, the gods would not be themselves if they did not pursue you with their envy. I have less reason to fear them."

"Ungrateful fellow!" interrupted his friend. "There will be numerous mortals to grudge you Helena. As for me, I have already felt many a slight foreboding; but we have already paid by no means a small tribute to the divine ones. The lamp is still burning in the sitting-room. Inform the sisters of their grandmother's death, and tell them the pleasant tidings you have brought us, but reserve until the morning a description of the terrible scenes you witnessed. We will not spoil their sleep. Mark my words! Helena's silent grief and her joy at our escape will lighten your heart."

And so it proved. True, Gorgias lived over again in his dreams the frightful spectacle witnessed the day before; but when the sun of the 2d day of August rose in full radiance over Alexandria and, early in the morning, boat after boat reached the Serpent Island, landing first Berenike and her nephews, the sons of the honoured philosopher Arius, then clients, officials, and friends of Dion, and former favourite guests of Barine, to greet the young pair and escort them from the refuge which had so long sheltered them back to the city and their midst, new and pleasant impressions robbed the gloomy picture of a large portion of its terrors.

"Tall Phryxus" had rapidly spread the news of the place where Dion and Barine had vanished, and that they had long been happily wedded. Many deemed it well worth a short voyage to see the actors in so strange an adventure and be the first to greet them. Besides, those who knew Barine and her husband were curious to learn how two persons accustomed to the life of a great capital had endured for months such complete solitude. Many feared or expected to see them emaciated and careworn, haggard or sunk in melancholy, and hence there were a number of astonished faces among those whose boats the freedman Pyrrhus guided as pilot through the shallows which protected his island.

The return of this rare couple to their home would have afforded an excellent opportunity for gay festivities. Sincerely as the majority of the populace mourned the fate of the Queen, and gravely as the more thoughtful feared for Alexandria's freedom under Roman rule, all rejoiced over the lenient treatment of the city. Their lives and property were safe, and the celebration of festivals had become a life habit with all classes. But the news of the death of Didymus's wife and the illness of the old man, who could not bear up under the loss of his faithful companion, gave Dion a right to refuse any gay welcome at his home.

Barine's sorrow was his also, and Didymus died a few days after his wife, with whom he had lived in the bonds of love for more than half a century —people said, "of a broken heart."

So Dion and his young wife entered his beautiful palace with no noisy festivities. Instead of the jubilant hymenæus, the voice of his own child greeted him on the threshold.

The mourning garments in which Barine welcomed him in the women's apartment reminded him of the envy of the gods which his friend had feared for him. But he often fancied that his mother's statue in the tablinum looked specially happy when the young mistress of the house entered it.

Barine, too, felt that her happiness as wife and mother in her magnificent home would have been overwhelming had not a wise destiny imposed upon her, just at this time, grief for those whom she loved.

Dion instantly devoted himself again to the affairs of the city and his own business. He and the woman he loved, who had first become really his own during a time of sore privation, had run into the harbour and gazed quietly at the storms of life. The anchor of love, which moored their ship to the solid earth, had been tested in the solitude of the Serpent Island.

CHAPTER XXIV.

THE fisherman and his family had watched the departure of their beloved guests with sorrowful hearts, and the women had shed many tears, although the sons of Pyrrhus had been dismissed from the fleet and were again helping their father at home, as in former times.

Besides, Dion had made the faithful freedman a prosperous man, and given his daughter, Dione, a marriage dowry. She was soon to become the wife of the captain of the Epicurus, Archibius's swift galley, whose acquaintance she had made when the vessel, on several occasions, brought Charmian's Nubian maid to the island. Anukis's object in making these visits was not only to see her friend, but to induce him to catch one of the poisonous serpents in the neighbouring island and keep it ready for the Queen.

Since Cleopatra had ascertained that no poison caused a less painful death than the fangs of the asp, she had resolved that the bite of one of these reptiles should release her from the burden of life. The clever Ethiopian had thought of inducing her friend Pyrrhus to procure the adder, but it had required all Aisopion's skill in persuasion, and the touching manner in which she understood how to describe the Queen's terrible situation and severe suffering, to conquer the reluctance of the upright man. At last she succeeded in persuading him to measure a queen by a different standard from a woman of the people, and inducing him to arrange the manner and time of conveying the serpent into the well-guarded palace. A signal was to inform him when the decisive hour arrived. After that he was to be ready with the asp in the fish-market every day. Probably his service would soon be claimed; for Octavianus's delay was scarcely an indication of a favourable decision of Cleopatra's fate.

True, she was permitted to live in royal state at Lochias, and had even been allowed to have the children, the twins, and little Alexander sent back to her with the promise that life and liberty would be granted them; but Cæsarion—whose treacherous tutor Rhodon lured him from the journey southward back to Alexandria by all sorts of representations, among them the return of Barine—was held prisoner in his father's temple, where he had sought refuge. This news, and the fact that Octavianus had condemned to death the youth who bore so striking a resemblance to Cæsar, had not remained concealed from the unhappy mother. She was also informed of the words in which the philosopher Arius had encouraged Cæsar's desire to rid himself of the son of his famous uncle. They referred to the Homeric saying concerning the disadvantage of having many rulers.

Everything which Cleopatra desired to know concerning events in the city reached her ears; for she was allowed much liberty—only she was closely watched day and night, and all the servants and officials to whom she granted an audience were carefully searched to keep from her all means of self-destruction.

True, it was very evident that she had closed her account with life. Her attempt to take no food and die of starvation must have been noticed. Threats directed against the children, through whom she could be most easily influenced, finally induced her to eat again. Octavianus was informed of all these things, and his conduct proved his anxiety to keep her from suicide.

Several Asiatic princes vied with each other in the desire to honour Mark Antony by a magnificent funeral, but Octavianus had allowed Cleopatra to provide the most superb obsequies. In the time of her deepest anguish it afforded her comfort and satisfaction to arrange everything herself, and even perform some offices with her own hands. The funeral had been as gorgeous as the dead man's love of splendour could have desired.

Iras and Charmian were often unable to understand how the Queen—who, since Antony's death, had suffered not only from the wounds she had inflicted upon herself in her despair, but also after her baffled attempt at starvation from a slow fever—had succeeded in resisting the severe exertions and mental agitation to which she had been subjected by Antony's funeral.

The return of Archibius with the children, however, had visibly reanimated her flagging energy.

She often went to Didymus's garden, which was now connected with the palace at Lochias, to watch their work and share whatever interested their young hearts.

But the gayest of mothers, who had understood how to enter so thoroughly into her children's pursuits, had now become a sorrowful, grave monitor. Though the lessons she urged upon them were often beautiful and wise, they were little suited to the ages of Archibius's pupils, for they usually referred to death and to questions of philosophy not easily understood by children.

She herself felt that she no longer struck the right key; but whenever she tried to change it and jest with them as usual, she could endure the forced gaiety only a short time; a painful revulsion, frequently accompanied by tears, followed, and she was obliged to leave her darlings.

The life her foe granted her seemed like an intrusive gift, an oppressive debt, which we desire to pay a troublesome creditor as soon as possible.

She seemed calmer and apparently content only

when permitted to talk with the companions of her youth concerning bygone days, or with them and Iras of death, and how it would be possible to put an end to an unwelcome existence.

After such conversations Iras and Charmian left her with bleeding hearts. They had long since resolved to share the fate of their royal mistress, whatever it might be. Their common suffering was the bond which again united them in affection. Iras had provided poisoned pins which had speedily destroyed the animals upon which they had been tried. Cleopatra knew of their existence, but she herself preferred the painless death bestowed by the serpent's bite, and it was long since her friends had seen the eyes of their beloved sovereign sparkle so brightly as when Charmian told her that a way had been found to obtain the uræus serpent as soon as it was needed. But it was not yet imperative to adopt the last expedient. Octavianus wished to be considered lenient, and perhaps might still be prevailed upon to grant the Queen and her children a future meet for their royal birth.

Cleopatra's reply was an incredulous smile, yet a faint hope which saved her from despair began to bud in her soul.

Dolabella, an aristocratic Roman, a scion of the noble Cornelius family, was in the Cæsar's train, and had been presented to the Egyptian Queen. In former years his father was a friend of Cleopatra;

nay, she had placed him under obligations by sending him, after the murder of Julius Cæsar, the military force at her command to be used against Cassius. True, her legions, by messengers from Dolabella himself, were despatched in another direction; but Cleopatra had not withdrawn her favour from Dolabella's father on that account. The latter had known her in Rome before the death of Cæsar, and had enthusiastically described the charms of the bewitching Egyptian sovereign. Though the youth found her only a mourning widow, ill in body and mind, he was so strongly attracted and deeply moved by her beauty, her brilliant intellect, her grace of bearing, her misfortunes and sufferings, that he devoted many hours to her, and would have considered it a happiness to render her greater services than circumstances permitted. He often accompanied her to the children, whose hearts had been completely won by his frank, cheerful nature; and so it happened that he soon became one of the most welcome guests at Lochias. He confided without reserve every feeling that stirred his soul to the warm-hearted woman who was so many years his senior, and through him she learned many things connected with Octavianus and his surroundings. Without permitting himself to be used as a tool, he became an advocate for the unfortunate woman whom he so deeply esteemed.

In intercourse with her he made every effort to inspire confidence in Octavianus, who favoured him, enjoyed his society, and in whose magnanimity the youth firmly believed.

He anticipated the best results from an interview between the Queen and the Cæsar; for he deemed it impossible that the successful conqueror could part untouched, and with no desire to mitigate her sad fate, from the woman who, in earlier years, had so fascinated his father, and whom he himself, though she might almost have been his mother, deemed peerless in her bewitching and gracious charm.

Cleopatra, on the contrary, shrank from meeting the man who had brought so much misfortune upon Mark Antony and herself, and inflicted upon her insults which were only too well calculated to make her doubt his clemency and truth. On the other hand, she could not deny Dolabella's assertion that it would be far less easy for Octavianus to refuse her in person the wishes she cherished for her children's future than through mediators. Proculejus had learned that Antony had named him to the Queen as the person most worthy of her confidence, and more keenly felt the wrong which, as the tool and obedient friend of Octavianus, he had inflicted upon the hapless woman. The memory of his unworthy deed, which history would chronicle, had robbed the sensitive man, the author and patron of budding Roman poetry, of many an hour's sleep, and therefore he also now laboured zealously to oblige the Queen and mitigate her hard fate. He, like the freedman Epaphroditus, who by Cæsar's orders watched carefully to prevent any attempt upon her life, seemed to base great hopes on such an interview, and endeavoured to persuade her to request an audience from the Cæsar.

Archibius said that, even in the worst case, it could not render the present state of affairs darker. Experience, he said to Charmian, proved that no man of any feeling could wholly resist the charm of her nature, and to him at least she had never seemed more winning than now. Who could have gazed unmoved into the beautiful face, so eloquent in its silent suffering, whose soul would not have been deeply touched by the sorrowful tones of her sweet voice? Besides, her sable mourning robes were so well suited to the slight tinge of melancholy which pervaded her whole aspect. When the fever flushed her cheeks, Archibius, spite of the ravages which grief, anxiety, and fear had made upon her charms, thought that he had never seen her look more beautiful. He knew her thoroughly, and was aware that her desire to follow the man she loved into the realm of death was sincere; nay, that it dominated her whole being. She clung to life only to die as soon as possible. The decision which, after her resolve to build the monument, she had recognized in the temple of Berenike as the right one, had become the rule of conduct of her life. Every thought, every conversation, led her back to the past. The future seemed to exist no longer. If Archibius succeeded in directing her thoughts to approaching days she occupied herself wholly with her children's fate. For herself she expected nothing, felt absolved from every duty except the one of protecting herself and her name from dishonour and humiliation.

The fact that Octavianus, when he doomed Cæsarion to death, permitted the other children to return to her with the assurance that no harm should befall them, proved that he made a distinction between them and his uncle's son, and had no fears that they threatened his own safety. She might expect important results in their favour from an interview with Octavianus, so she at last authorized Proculejus to request an audience.

The Imperator's answer came the very same day. It was his place to seek her—so ran the Cæsar's message. This meeting must decide her fate. Cleopatra was aware of this, and begged Charmian to remember the asp.

Her attendants had been forbidden to leave Lochias, but Epaphroditus permitted them to receive visitors. The Nubian's merry, amusing talk had made friends for her among the Roman guards, who allowed her to pass in and out unmolested. On her return, of course, she was searched with the utmost care, like every one who entered Lochias.

The decisive hour was close at hand. Charmian knew what she must do in any event, but there was still one desire for whose fulfilment she longed. She wished to greet Barine and see her boy.

To spare Iras, she had hitherto refrained from sending for Dion's wife. The sight of the mother and child might have reopened wounds still unhealed, and she would not inflict this sorrow upon her niece, who for a long time had once more been loyally devoted to her.

Octavianus did not hasten to fulfil his assurance. But, at the end of a week, Proculejus brought the news that he could promise a visit from the Cæsar that afternoon. The Queen was deeply agitated, and desired before the interview to pay a visit to her tomb. Iras offered to accompany her, and as Cleopatra intended to remain an hour or longer, Charmian thought it a favourable opportunity to see Barine and her boy.

Dion's wife had been informed of her friend's wish, and Anukis, who was to take her to Lochias, did not wait long for the mother and child.

Didymus's garden—now the property of the royal children—was the scene of the meeting. In the shade of the familiar trees the young mother sank upon the breast of her faithful friend, and Charmian could not gaze her fill at the boy, or weary of tracing in his features a resemblance to his grandfather Leonax.

How much these two women, to whom Fate had

allotted lives so widely different, found to tell each other! The older felt transported to the past, the younger seemed to have naught save a present rich in blessing and a future green with hope. She had good news to tell of her sister also. Helena had long been the happy wife of Gorgias who, however, spite of the love with which he surrounded the young mistress of his house, numbered among his most blissful hours those which were devoted to overseeing the progress of the work on the mausoleum, where he met Cleopatra.

Time flew swiftly to the two women, and it was a painful surprise when one of the eunuchs on guard announced that the Queen had returned. Again Charmian embraced her lover's grandson, blessed him and the young mother, sent messages of remembrance to Dion, begged Barine to think of her affectionately when she had passed from earth and, if her heart prompted her to the act, to anoint or adorn with a ribbon or flower the tombstone of the woman who had no friend to render her such a service.

Deeply moved by the firmness with which Charmian witnessed the approach of death, Barine listened in silence, but suddenly started as the sharp tones of a well-known voice called her friend's name and, as she turned, Iras stood before her. Pallid and emaciated, she looked in her long, floating black robes the very incarnation of misery.

The sight pierced the heart of the happy wife and mother. She felt as if much of the joy which Iras lacked had fallen to her own lot, and all the grief and woe she had ever endured had been transferred to her foe. She would fain have approached humbly and said something very kind and friendly; but when she saw the tall, haggard woman gazing at her child, and noticed the disagreeable expression which had formerly induced her to compare her to a sharp thorn, a terrible dread of this woman's evil eye which might harm her boy seized the mother's heart and, overwhelmed by an impulse beyond control, she covered his face with her own veil.

Iras saw it, and after Barine had answered her question, "Dion's child?" in the affirmative, with a glance beseeching forbearance, the girl drew up her slender figure, saying with arrogant coldness: "What do I care for the child? We have more important matters on our hearts."

Then she turned to Charmian to inform her, in the tone of an official announcement, that during the approaching interview the Queen desired her attendance also.

Octavianus had appointed sunset for the interview, and it still lacked several hours of the time. The suffering Queen felt wearied by her visit to the mausoleum, where she had implored the spirit of Antony, if he had any power over the conqueror's heart, to induce him to release her from this torturing uncertainty and promise the children a happy fate.

To Dolabella, who had accompanied her from the tomb to the palace, she said that she expected only one thing from this meeting, and then won from him a promise which strengthened her courage and seemed the most precious boon which could be granted at this time.

She had expressed the fear that Octavianus would still leave her in doubt. The youth spoke vehemently in Cæsar's defence, and closed with the exclamation, "If he should still keep you in suspense, he would be not only cool and circumspect——"

"Then," Cleopatra interrupted, "be nobler, be less cruel, and release your father's friend from these tortures. If he does not reveal to me what awaits me and you learn it, then—you will not say no, you cannot refuse me—then you, yes, you will inform me?"

Promptly and firmly came the reply: "What have I been able to do for you until now? But I will release you from *this* torture, if possible." Then he hastily turned his back, that he might not be compelled to see the eunuchs stationed at the palace gate search the garments of the royal captive.

His promise sustained the failing courage of the wearied, anxious Queen, and she reclined upon the cushions of a lounge to recover from the exhausting expedition; but she had scarcely closed her eyes when the pavement of the court-yard rang under the hoofs of the four horses which bore the Cæsar to Lochias. Cleopatra had not expected the visit so early.

She had just been consulting with her attendants about the best mode of receiving him. At first she had been disposed to do so on the throne, clad in her royal attire, but she afterwards thought that she was too ill and weak to bear the heavy ornaments. Besides, the man and successful conqueror would show himself more indulgent and gracious to the suffering woman than to the princess.

There was much to palliate the course which she had pursued in former days, and she had carefully planned the defence by which she hoped to influence his calm but not unjust nature. Many things in her favour were contained in the letters from Cæsar and Antony which, after her husband's death, she had read again and again during so many wakeful nights, and they had just been brought to her.

Both Archibius and the Roman Proculejus had counselled her not to receive him entirely alone. The latter did not express his opinion in words, but he knew that Octavianus was more readily induced to noble and lenient deeds when there was no lack of witnesses to report them to the world. It was advisable to provide spectators for the most consummate actor of his day.

Therefore the Queen had retained Iras, Charmian, and some of the officials nearest to her person, among them the steward Seleukus, who could give information if any question arose concerning the delivery of the treasure.

She had also intended, after she had somewhat recovered from the visit to the tomb, to be robed in fresh garments. This was prevented by the Cæsar's unexpected arrival. Now, even had time permitted, she would have been unable to have her hair arranged, she felt so weak and yet so feverishly excited.

The blood coursed hotly through her veins and flushed her cheeks. When told that the Cæsar was close at hand, she had only time to raise herself a little higher on her cushions, push back her hair, and let Iras, with a few hasty touches, adjust the folds of her mourning robes. Had she attempted to advance to meet him, her limbs would have failed to support her.

When the Cæsar at last entered, she could greet him only by a wave of her hand; but Octavianus, who had uttered the usual salutations from the threshold, quickly broke the painful silence, saying with a courteous bow:

"You summoned me—I came. Every one is subject to beauty—even the victor."

Cleopatra's head drooped in shame as she answered distinctly, yet in a tone of modest denial:

"I only asked the favour of an audience. I did

not *summon*. I thank you for granting the request. If it is dangerous for man to bow to woman's charms, no peril threatens you here. Beauty cannot withstand tortures such as those which have been imposed on me—barely can life remain. But you prevented my casting it from me. If you are just, you will grant to the woman whom you would not permit to die an existence whose burden will not exceed her power to endure."

The Cæsar again bowed silently and answered courteously:

"I intend to make it worthy of you."

"Then," cried Cleopatra impetuously, "release me from this torturing uncertainty. You are not one of the men who never look beyond to-day and to-morrow."

"You are thinking," said Octavianus harshly, "of one who perhaps would still be among us, if with wiser caution——"

Cleopatra's eyes, which hitherto had met the victor's cold gaze with modest entreaty, flashed angrily, and a majestic: "Let the past rest!" interrupted him.

But she soon mastered the indignation which had stirred her passionate blood, and in a totally different tone, not wholly free from gentle persuasion, she continued:

"The provident intellect of the man whose nod the universe obeys grasps the future as well as the present. Must not he, therefore, have decided the children's fate ere he consented to see their mother? The only obstacle in your path, the son of your great uncle——"

"His doom was a necessity," interrupted the conqueror in a tone of sincere regret. "As I mourned Antony, I grieve for the unfortunate boy."

"If that is true," replied Cleopatra eagerly, "it does honour to the kindness of your heart. When Proculejus wrested the dagger from my grasp he blamed me because I attributed to the most clement of conquerors harshness and implacability."

"Two qualities," the Cæsar protested, "which are wholly alien to my nature."

"And which—even if you possessed them—you neither could nor ought to use," cried Cleopatra, "if you really mean the beautiful words you so often utter that, as the nephew and heir of the great Julius Cæsar, you intend to walk in his footsteps. Cæsarion—there is his bust—was the image in every feature of his father, your illustrious model. To me, the hapless woman now awaiting my sentence from his nephew's lips, the gods granted, as the most precious of all gifts, the love of your divine uncle. And what love! The world knew not what I was to his great heart, but my wish to defend myself from misconception bids me show it to you, his heir. From you I expect my sentence. You are the judge. These letters are my strongest defence. I rely upon them to show myself to you as I was and am, not as envy and slander describe me.—The little ivory casket, Iras! It contains the precious proofs of Cæsar's love, his letters to me."

She raised the lid with trembling hands and, as these mementoes carried her back to the past, she continued in lower tones:

"Among all my treasures this simple little coffer has been for half a lifetime my most valued jewel. He gave it to me. It was in the midst of the fierce contest here at the Bruchium."

Then, while unfolding the first roll, she directed Octavianus's attention to it and the remainder of the contents of the little casket, exclaiming:

"Silent pages, yet how eloquent! Each one a peerless picture, the powerful thinker, the man of action, who permits his restless intellect to repose, and suffers his heart to overflow with the love of youth! Were I vain, Octavianus, I might call each one of these letters a trophy of victory, an Olympic garland. The woman to whom Julius Cæsar owned his subjugation might well hold her head higher than the unhappy, vanquished Queen who, save the permission to die——"

"Do not part with the letters," said Octavianus kindly. "Who can doubt that they are a precious treasure——"

"The most precious and at the same time the advocate of the accused," replied Cleopatra eagerly; "on them—as you have already heard—rests my vindication. I will commence with their contents. How terrible it is to make what is sacred to us and intended only to elevate our own hearts serve a purpose, to do what has always been repugnant to us! But I need an advocate and, Octavianus, these letters will restore to the wretched, suffering beggar the dignity and majesty of the Queen. The world knows but two powers to which Julius Cæsar bowed—the thrall of the pitiable woman on this couch, and of all-conquering death. An unpleasant fellowship—but I do not shrink from it; for death robbed him of life, and from my hand—— I ask only a brief moment. How gladly I would spare myself my own praises, and you the necessity of listening to them! Yes, here it is: 'Through you, you irresistible woman,' he writes, 'I learned for the first time, after youth was over, how beautiful life can be.'"

Cleopatra, as she spoke, handed Cæsar the letter. But while she was still searching hastily for another he returned the first, saying:

"I understand only too well your reluctance to allow such confidential effusions to play the part of defender. I can imagine their purport, and they shall influence me as if I had read them all. However eloquent they may be, they are needless witnesses. Is any written testimony required in behalf of charms whose magic is still potent?"

A bewitching smile, which seemed like a confirmation of the haughty young conqueror's flattering words, flitted over Cleopatra's face.

Octavianus noticed it. This woman indeed possessed enthralling charms, and he felt the slight flush that suffused his cheeks.

This unhappy captive, this suffering supplicant, could still draw into her net any man who did not possess the cool watchfulness which panoplied his soul. Was it the marvellous melody of her voice, the changeful lustre of her tearful eyes, the aristocratic grace of the noble figure, the exquisite symmetry of the hands and feet, the weakness of the prostrate sufferer, strangely blended with truly royal majesty, or the thought that love for her had bound earth's greatest and loftiest men with indissoluble fetters, which lent this fragile woman, who had long since passed the boundaries of youth, so powerful a spell of attraction?

At any rate, however certain of himself he might be, he must guard his feelings. He understood how to bridle passion far better than the uncle who was so greatly his superior.

Yet it was of the utmost importance to keep her alive, and therefore to maintain her belief in his admiration. He wished to show the world and the Great Queen of the East, who had just boasted of conquering, like death, even the most mighty, his own supremacy as man and victor. But he must also be gentle, in order not to endanger the object for which he wanted her. She must accompany him to Rome. She and her children promised to render his triumph the most brilliant and memorable one which any conqueror had ever displayed to the senate and the people. In a light tone which, however, revealed the emotion of his soul, he answered: "My illustrious uncle was known as a friend of fair women. His stern life was crowned with flowers by many hands, and he acknowledged these favours verbally and perhaps—as he did to you in all these letters—with the reed. His genius was greater, at any rate more many-sided and mobile, than mine. He succeeded, too, in pursuing different objects at the same time with equal devotion. I am wholly absorbed in the cares of state, of government, and war. I feel grateful when I can permit our poets to adorn my leisure for a brief space. Overburdened with toil, I have no time to yield myself captive, as my uncle did in these very rooms, to the most charming of women. If I could follow my own will, you would be the first from whom I would seek the gifts of Eros.—But it may not be! We Romans learn to curb even the most ardent wishes when duty and morality command. There is no city in the world where half so many gods are worshipped as here; and what strange deities are numbered among them! It needs a special effort of the intellect to understand them. But the simple duties of the domestic hearth!—they are too prosaic for you Alexandrians, who imbibe philosophy with your mothers' milk. What marvel, if I looked for them in vain? True, they would find little satisfaction —our household gods I mean—here, where the rigid demands of Hymen are mute before the ardent pleadings of Eros. Marriage is scarcely reckoned among the sacred things of life. But this opinion seems to displease you."

"Because it is false," cried Cleopatra, repressing with difficulty a fresh outburst of indignation. "Yet, if I see aright, your reproach is aimed only at the bond which united me to the man who was called your sister's husband. But I will—— I would gladly remain silent, but you force me to speak, and I will do so, though your own friend, Proculejus, is signing to me to be cautious. I—I, Cleopatra, was the wife of Mark Antony according to the customs of this country, when you wedded him to the widow of Marcellus, who had scarcely closed his eyes. Not she, but I, was the deserted wife—I to whom his heart belonged until the hour of his death, not the unloved consort wedded——" Here her voice fell. She had yielded to the passionate impulse which urged her to express her feelings in the matter, and now continued in a tone of gentle explanation: "I know that you proposed this alliance solely for the peace and welfare of Rome——"

"To guard both, and to spare the blood of tens of thousands," Octavianus added with proud decision. "Your clear brain perceived the true state of affairs. If, spite of the grave importance of these motives, you—— But what voices would not that of the heart silence with you women! The man, the Roman, succeeded in closing his ears to its siren song. Were it otherwise, I would never have chosen for my sister a husband by whom I knew her happiness would be so ill-guarded—I would, as I have already said, be unable to master my own admiration of the loveliest of women. But I ought scarcely to boast of that. I fear that a heart like yours opens less quickly to the modest Octavianus than to a Julius Cæsar or the brilliant Mark Antony. Yet I may be permitted to confess that perhaps I might have avoided conducting this unhappy war against my friend to the end under my own guidance, and appearing myself in Egypt, had I not been urged by the longing to see once more the woman who had dazzled my boyish eyes. Now, in my mature manhood, I desired to comprehend those marvellous gifts of mind, that matchless sagacity——"

"Sagacity!" interrupted the Queen, shrugging her shoulders mournfully. "You possess a far greater share of what is commonly called by that name. My fate proves it. The pliant intellect which the gods bestowed on me would ill sustain the test in this hour of anguish. But if you really care to learn what mental power Cleopatra once possessed, relieve me of this terrible burden of uncertainty, and grant me a position in life which will permit my paralyzed soul to move freely once more."

"It depends solely on yourself," Octavianus eagerly responded, "to make your future life, not only free from care, but beautiful."

"On me?" asked Cleopatra in astonishment. "Our weal and woe are in your hands alone. I am modest and ask nothing save to know what you intend for our future, what you mean by the lot which you term beautiful."

"Nothing less," replied the Cæsar quietly, "than what seems to lie nearest to your own heart—a life of that freedom of soul to which you aspire."

The breath of the agitated Queen began to come more quickly and, no longer able to control the impatience which overpowered her, she exclaimed, "With the assurance of your favour on your lips, you refuse to discuss the question which interests, me beyond any other—for which, if any, you must have been prepared when you came here——"

"Reproaches?" asked Octavianus with well-feigned surprise. "Would it not rather be my place to complain? It is precisely because I am so thoroughly sincere in the friendly disposition which you read aright from my words, that some of your measures cannot fail to wound me. Your treasures were to be committed to the flames. It would be unfair to expect tokens of friendship from the vanquished; but can you deny that even the bitterest hatred could scarcely succeed in devising anything more hostile?"

"Let the past rest! Who would not seek in war to diminish the enemy's booty?" pleaded the Queen in a soothing tone. But as Octavianus delayed his answer, she continued more eagerly: "It is said that the ibex in the mountains, when in mortal peril, rushes upon the hunter and hurls him with it down the precipice. The same impulse is natural to human beings, and praiseworthy, I think, in both. Forget the past, as I will try to do, I repeat with uplifted hands. Say that you will permit the sons whom I gave to Antony to ascend the Egyptian throne, not under their mother's guardianship, but that of Rome, and grant me freedom wherever I may live, and I will gladly transfer to you, down to the veriest trifles, all the property and treasures I possess."

She clenched her little hand impatiently under the folds of her robe as she spoke; but Octavianus lowered his eyes, saying carelessly: "In war the victor disposes of the property of the vanquished; but my heart restrains me from applying the universal law to you, who are so far above ordinary mortals. Your wealth is said to be vast, though the foolish war which Antony, with your aid, so greatly prolonged, devoured vast sums. In this country squandered gold seems like the grass which, when mowed, springs up anew."

"You speak," replied Cleopatra, more and more deeply incensed, with proud composure, "of the treasures which my ancestors, the powerful monarchs of a wealthy country, amassed during three hundred years for their noble race and for the adornment of the women of their line. Parsimony did not accord with the generosity and lofty nature of an Antony, yet avarice itself would not deem the portion still remaining insignificant. Every article is registered."

While speaking, she took a manuscript from the hand of Seleukus and passed it to Octavianus who, with a slight bend of the head, received it in silence. But he had scarcely begun to read it when the steward, a little corpulent man with twinkling eyes half buried in his fat cheeks, raised his short forefinger, pointed insolently at the Queen, and asserted that she was trying to conceal some things, and had ordered him not to place them on the list. Every tinge of colour faded from the lips and cheeks of the agitated and passionate woman; tortured by feverish impatience and no longer able to control her emotions, she raised herself and, with her own dainty hand, struck the accuser—whom she had lifted from poverty and obscurity to his present high position—again and again in the face, till Octavianus, with a smile of superiority, begged her, much as the man deserved his punishment, to desist.

The unfortunate woman, thus thrown off her

guard, flung herself back on her couch and, panting for breath, with tears streaming from her eyes, sobbed aloud, declaring that in the presence of such unendurable insult, such contemptible baseness, she fairly loathed herself. Then pressing her clenched hands upon her temples, she exclaimed: "Before the eyes of the foe my royal dignity, which I have maintained all my life, falls from me like a borrowed mantle. Yet what am I? What shall I be to-morrow, what later? But who beneath the sun who has warm blood in his veins can preserve his composure when juicy grapes are held before his thirsting lips to be withdrawn, as from Tantalus, ere he can taste them? You came hither with the assurance of your favour; but the flattering words of promise which you bestowed upon the unhappy woman were probably only the drops of poppy-juice given to soothe the ravings of fever. Was the favour which you permitted me to see and anticipate for the future merely intended to delude a miserable——"

But she went no further; Octavianus, with dignified bearing and loud, clear tones, interrupted: "Whoever believes the heir of Cæsar capable of shamefully deceiving a noble woman, a queen, the object of his illustrious uncle's love, insults and wounds him; but the just anger which overmastered you may serve as your apology. Ay," he added in a totally different tone, "I might even have cause to be grateful for this indignation, and to wish for another opportunity to witness the outbreak of passion though in its unbridled fierceness —the royal lioness is scarcely aware of her own beauty when the tempest of wrath sweeps her away. What must she be when it is love that constrains the flame of her glowing soul to burst into a blaze?"

"Her glowing soul!" Cleopatra eagerly repeated, and the desire awoke to subjugate this man who had so confidently boasted of his power of resistance. Though he might be stronger than many others, he certainly was not invincible. And aware of her still unbroken sway over the hearts of men, her eyes sparkled with the alluring radiance of love, and a bewitching smile brightened her face.

The young Imperator's heart began to chafe under the curb and to beat more quickly, his cheeks flushed and paled by turns. How she gazed at him! What if she loved the nephew as she had once loved the uncle who, through her, had learned what bliss life can offer? Ay, it must be happiness to kiss those lips, to be clasped in those exquisite arms, to hear one's own name tenderly spoken by those musical tones. Even the magnificent marble statue of Ariadne, which he had seen in Athens, had not displayed to his gaze lines more beautiful than those of the woman reclining on yonder pillows. Who could venture to speak in her presence of vanished charms? Ah, no! The spell which had conquered Julius Cæsar was as vivid, as potent as ever. He himself felt its power; he was young, and after such unremitting exertions he too yearned to quaff the nectar of the noblest joys, to steep body and soul in peerless bliss.

So, with a hasty movement, he took one step towards her couch, resolved to grasp her hands and raise them to his lips. His ardent gaze answered hers; but surprised by the power which, though so heavily burdened with physical and mental suffering, she still possessed over the strongest and coldest of men, she perceived what was passing in his soul, and a smile of triumph, blended with the most bitter contempt, hovered around her beautiful lips. Should she dupe him into granting her wishes by feigning love for the first time? Should she yield to the man who had insulted her, in order to induce him to accord the children their rights? Should she, to gratify her lover's foe, relinquish the sacred grief which was drawing her after him, give posterity and her children the right to call her, instead of the most loyal of the loyal, a dishonoured woman, who sold herself for power?

To all these questions came a prompt denial. The single stride which Octavianus had made towards her, his eyes aflame with love, gave her the right to feel that she had vanquished the victor, and the proud delight of triumph was too plainly reflected in her mobile features to escape the penetrating, distrustful gaze of the subjugated Cæsar.

But he had scarcely perceived what threatened him, and remembered her words concerning his famous uncle's surrender only to her and to death, when he succeeded in conquering his quickly kindled senses. Blushing at his own weakness, he averted his eyes from the Queen, and when he met those of Proculejus and the other witnesses of the scene, he realized the abyss on whose verge he stood. He had half succumbed to the danger of losing, by a moment's weakness, the fruit of great sacrifices and severe exertions.

His expressive eyes, which had just rested rapturously upon a beautiful woman, now scanned the spectators with the stern glance of a monarch and, apparently wishing to moderate an excess of flattering recognition which might be misinterpreted, he said in an almost pedagogical tone:

"Yet we would rather see the noble lioness in the majestic repose which best suits all sovereigns. It is difficult for a calm, deliberate nature like mine to understand an ardent, quickly kindling heart."

Cleopatra had watched this sudden transition with more surprise than disappointment. Octavianus had half surrendered to her, but recovered his self-command in time, and a man of his temperament does not readily succumb twice to a danger which he barely escaped. And this was well! He should learn that he had misunderstood the glance which fired his heart; so she answered distantly, with majestic dignity:

"Misery such as mine quenches all ardour. And love? Woman's heart is ever open to it, save where it has lost the desire for power and pleasure. You are young and happy, therefore your soul still yearns for love—I know that—though not for mine. To me, on the contrary, one suitor only is welcome, he with the lowered torch, whom you keep aloof from me. With him alone is to be found the boon for which this soul has longed from childhood—painless peace! You smile. My past gives you the right to do so. I will not lessen it. Each individual lives his or her own life. Few understand the changes of their own existence, far less those of a stranger's. The world has witnessed how Peace fled from my path, or I from hers, and yet I see the possibility of finding the way. I am safe from the only things which would debar me from those joys—humiliation and disgrace." Here she hesitated; then, as if in explanation, continued in the sweetest tones at her command: "Your generosity, I think, will guard from these two foes the woman whom just now—I did not fail to see it—you considered worthy of a more than gracious glance. I shall treasure it among memories which will never fade. But now, illustrious Imperator! tell me, what is your decision concerning me and the children? What may we hope from your favour?"

"That Octavianus will be more and more warmly animated by the desire to accord you and yours a worthy destiny, the more firmly you expect that he will attest his generosity."

"And if I fulfil this desire and expect from you everything that is great and noble—the condition is not difficult—what proofs of your graciousness will then await us?"

"Paint them with all the fervour of that vivid power of imagination which interpreted even my glance in your favour, and devised the marvels by which you rendered the greatest and most brilliant man in Rome the happiest of mortals. But—by Zeus!—it is the fourth hour after noonday!"

A glance from the window had caused the exclamation. Then, pressing his hand upon his heart, he continued in a tone of the most sincere regret: "How gladly I would prolong this fascinating conversation, but important matters which, unfortunately, cannot be deferred, summon me———"

"And your answer?" cried Cleopatra, panting for breath and gazing at him with eyes full of expectation.

"Must I repeat it?" he asked with impatient haste. "Very well, then. In return for implicit confidence on your part, favour, forgiveness, cordiality, every consideration which you can justly desire. Your heart is so rich in warmth of feeling, grant me but a small share of it and ask tangible gifts in return. They are already bestowed." Then greeting her like a friend who is reluctant to say farewell, he hastily left the apartment.

"Gone—gone!" cried Iras as the door closed behind him. "An eel that slips from the hand which strives to hold him."

"Northern ice," added Cleopatra gloomily as Charmian aided her to find a more comfortable position. "As smooth as it is cold; there is nothing more to hope."

"Yes, my royal mistress, yes," Iras eagerly protested. "Dolabella is waiting for him in the Philadelphus court-yard. From him—you have his promise—we shall learn what Octavianus has in store for you."

In truth, the Cæsar did find the youth at the first gate of the palace, inspecting his superb Cyrenean horses.

"Magnificent animals!" cried Octavianus; "a gift from the city! Will you drive with me?—A remarkable, a very remarkable woman!"

"Isn't she?" asked Dolabella eagerly.

"Undoubtedly," replied the Cæsar. "But though she might almost be your mother, an uncommonly dangerous one for youths of your age. What a melting voice, what versatility, what fervour! And yet such regal grace in every movement! But I wish to stifle, not to fan, the spark which perhaps has already fallen into your heart. And the play, the farce which she just enacted before me in the midst of most serious matters!"

He uttered a low, short laugh; but Dolabella exclaimed expectantly: "You rarely laugh, but this conversation—apparently—excites your mirth. So the result was satisfactory?"

"Let us hope so. I was as gracious to her as possible."

"That is delightful. May I know in what manner your kindness and wisdom have shaped her future? Or, rather, what did you promise the vanquished Queen?"

"My favour, if she will trust me."

"Proculejus and I will continue to strengthen her confidence. And if we succeed——?"

"Then, as I have said, she will have my favour—a generous abundance of favour."

"But her future destiny? What fate will you bestow on her and her children?"

"Whatever the degree of her confidence deserves."

Here he hesitated, for he met Dolabella's earnest, troubled gaze, which was blended with a shade of reproach.

Octavianus desired to retain the enthusiastic admiration of the youth, who perhaps was destined to lofty achievements, so he continued in a confidential tone: "To you, my young friend, I can venture to speak more frankly. I will gladly grant the most aspiring wishes of this fascinating and, I repeat, very remarkable woman, but first I need her for my triumph. The Romans would have cause to reproach me if I deprived them of the sight of this Queen, this peerless woman, in many respects the first of her time. We shall soon set out for Syria. The Queen and her children I shall send in three days to Rome. If, in the triumphal procession there, she creates the sensation I anticipate from a spectacle so worthy of admiration, she shall learn how I reward those who oblige me."

Dolabella had listened in silence. When the Cæsar entered the carriage, he requested permission to remain behind.

Octavianus drove alone eastward to the camp where, in the vicinity of the Hippodrome, men were surveying the ground on which the suburb of Nikopolis—city of victory—was to be built to commemorate for future generations the victory of the first Emperor over Antony and Cleopatra. It grew, but never attained any great importance.

The noble Cornelius gazed indignantly after his sovereign's fiery steeds; then, drawing up his stately figure to its full height, he entered the palace with a firm step. The act might cost him his life, but he would do what he believed to be his duty to the noble woman who had honoured him with her friendship. This rare sovereign was too good to feast the eyes of the rabble.

A few minutes later Cleopatra knew her impending ignominy.

CHAPTER XXV.

THE next morning the Queen had many whispered conversations with Charmian, and the latter with Anukis. The day before, Archibius's gardener had brought to his master's sister some unusually fine figs, which grew in the old garden of Epicurus. This fruit was also mentioned, and Anukis went to Kanopus, and thence, in the steward's carriage, with a basket of the very best ones to the fish-market. There she had a great deal to say to Pyrrhus, and the freedman went to his boat with the figs.

Shortly after the Nubian's return the Queen came back to the palace from the mausoleum. Her features bore an impress of resolution usually alien to them; nay, the firmly compressed lips gave them an expression of actual sternness. She knew what duty required, and regarded her approaching end as an inevitable necessity. Death seemed to her like a journey which she must take in order to escape the most terrible disgrace. Besides, life after the death of Antony was no longer the same; it had been only a tiresome delay and waiting for the children's sake.

The visit to the tomb had been intended, as it were, to announce her coming to her husband. She had remained a long time in the silent hall, where she had garlanded the coffin with flowers, kissed it, talked to the dead man as if he were still alive, and told him that the day had come when what he had mentioned in his will as the warmest desire of his heart—to rest beside her in the same tomb—would be fulfilled. Among the thousand forms of suffering which had assailed her, nothing had seemed so hard to bear as to be deprived of his society and love.

Then she had gone into the garden, embraced and kissed the children, and entreated them to remember her tenderly. Her purpose had not been concealed from Archibius, but Charmian had told him the menace of the future, and he approved her decision. By the exertion of all his innate strength of will, he succeeded in concealing the grief which rent his faithful heart. She must die. The thought of seeing her adorn the triumphal procession of Octavianus was unbearable to him also. Her thanks and entreaties to be an affectionate guardian to the children were received with an external calmness which afterwards seemed to him utterly incomprehensible.

When she spoke of her approaching meeting with her lover, he asked whether she had entirely abandoned the teachings of Epicurus, who believed that death absolutely ended existence.

Cleopatra eagerly assented, saying: "Absence of pain has ceased to appear to me the chief earthly blessing, since I have known that love does not bring pleasure only, since I have learned that pain is the inseparable companion of love. I will not give it up, nor will I part from my lover. Whoever experiences what fate has allotted to me has learned to know other gods than those whom the master described as dwelling happily in undisturbed repose. Rather eternal torture in another world, united to the man I love, than painless, joyless mere existence in a desolate, incomprehensible, unknown region! You will be the last to teach the children to yearn for freedom from pain———"

"Because, like you," cried Archibius, "I have learned how great a blessing is love, and that love is pain."

As he spoke he bent over her hand to kiss it, but she took his temples between her hands and, bending hastily, pressed her lips on his broad brow.

Then his self-control vanished, and, sobbing aloud, he hurried back to the children.

Cleopatra gazed after him with a sorrowful smile, and leaning on Charmian's arm, she entered the palace.

There she was bathed and, robed in costly mourning garments, reclined among her cushions to take breakfast, which was usually served at this hour.

Iras and Charmian shared it.

When dessert was carried in, the Nubian brought a basket filled with delicious figs. A peasant, she told Epaphroditus, who was watching the meal, had given them to her because they were so remarkably fine. Some had already been snatched by the guards.

The Queen and her companions ate a little of the fruit, and Proculejus, who had come to greet Cleopatra, was also persuaded to taste one of the finest figs.

At the end of the meal Cleopatra wished to rest.

The Roman gentlemen and the guards retired.

At last the women were alone, and gazed at each other silently.

Charmian timidly lifted the upper layer of the fruit, but the Queen said mournfully:

"The wife of Antony dragged through the streets of Rome behind the victor's chariot, a spectacle for the populace and envious matrons!" Then, starting up, she exclaimed: "What a thought! Was it too great for Octavianus, or too petty? He who so loudly boasts his knowledge of mankind expects this impossibility from the woman who revealed her inmost soul to him as fully as he concealed his from her. We will show him how small is his comprehension of human nature, and teach him modesty."

A contemptuous smile flitted over her beautiful lips as, with rapid movements, she flung handful after handful of figs on the table, till she saw something stirring under the fruit, and with a sigh of relief exclaimed under her breath:

"There it is!" as with hasty resolution she held out her arm towards the asp, which hissed at her.

While gazing intently at the movements of the viper, which seemed afraid to fulfil the dread office, she said to her attendants:

"I thank you—thank you for everything. Be calm. You know, Iras, it will cause no pain. They say it is like falling asleep." Then she shuddered slightly, adding: "Death is a solemn thing; yet it must be. Why does the serpent delay? There—there; I will keep firm. Ambition and love were the moving forces of my life. Men shall praise my memory.—I follow you, Mark Antony!"

Charmian bent over the left arm of her royal mistress, which hung loosely at her side, and, weeping aloud, covered it with kisses, while Cleopatra, watching the motions of the asp still more closely, added:

"The peace of our garden of Epicurus will begin to-day. Whether it will be painless, who can tell? Yet—there I agree with Archibius—life's greatest joy—love—is blended with pain, as yonder branch of exquisite roses from Dolabella, the last gift of friendship, has its sharp thorns. I think you have both experienced this. The twins and my little darling—— When they think of their mother and her end, will not the children——"

Here she uttered a low cry. The asp had struck its fangs into the upper part of her arm like an icy flash of lightning, and a few instants later Cleopatra sank back upon her pillows lifeless.

Iras, pale but calm, pointed to her, saying: "Like a sleeping child. Bewitching even in death. Fate itself was constrained to do her will and fulfil the last desire of the great Queen, the victorious woman, whom no heart resisted. Its decree shatters the presumptuous plan of Octavianus. The victor will show himself to the Romans without thee, thou dear one."

Sobbing violently, she bent over the inanimate form, closed the eyes, and kissed the lips and brow. The weeping Charmian did the same.

Then the footsteps of men were heard in the anteroom, and Iras, who was the first to notice them, cried eagerly:

"The moment is approaching! I am glad it is close at hand. Does it not seem to you also as if the very sun in the heavens was darkened?"

Charmian nodded assent, and whispered, "The poison?"

"Here!" replied Iras calmly, holding out a plain pin. "One little prick, and the deed will be done. Look! But no. You once inflicted the deepest suffering upon me. You know—Dion, the playmate of my childhood—— It is forgiven. But now—you will do me a kindness. You will spare my using the pin myself. Will you not? I will repay you. If you wish, my hand shall render you the same service."

Charmian clasped her niece to her heart, kissed her, pricked her arm lightly, and gave her the other pin, saying:

"Now it is your turn. Our hearts were filled with love for one who understood how to bestow it as none other ever did, and our love was returned. What matters all else that we sacrificed? Those on whom the sun shines need no other light. Love is pain," she said in dying, "but this pain—especially that of renunciation for love's sake—bears with it a joy, an exquisite joy, which renders death easy. To me it seems as if it were merely following the Queen to—— Oh, that hurt!"

Iras's pin had pricked her.

The poison did its work quickly. Iras was seized with giddiness, and could scarcely stand. Charmian had just sunk on her knees, when some one knocked loudly at the closed door, and the voices of Epaphroditus and Proculejus imperiously demanded admittance.

When no answer followed, the lock was hastily burst open.

Charmian was found lying pale and distorted at the feet of her royal mistress; but Iras, tottering and half stupefied by the poison, was adjusting the diadem, which had slipped from its place. To keep from her beloved Queen everything that could detract from her beauty had been her last care.

Enraged, fairly frantic with wrath, the Romans rushed towards the women. Epaphroditus had seen Iras still occupied in arranging Cleopatra's ornaments. Now he endeavoured to raise her companion, saying reproachfully, "Charmian, was this well done?" Summoning her last strength, she answered in a faltering voice, "Perfectly well, and worthy a descendant of Egyptian kings." Her eyes closed, but Proculejus, the author, who had gazed long with deep emotion into the beautiful proud face of the Queen whom he had so greatly wronged, said: "No other woman on earth was ever so admired by the greatest, so loved by the loftiest. Her fame echoed from nation to nation throughout the world. It will continue to resound from generation to generation; but however loudly men may extol the bewitching charm, the fervour of the love which survived death, her intellect, her knowledge, the heroic courage with which she preferred the tomb to ignominy—the praise of these two must not be forgotten. Their fidelity deserves it. By their marvellous end they unconsciously erected the most beautiful monument to their mistress; for what genuine goodness and lovableness must have been possessed by the woman who, after the greatest reverses, made it seem more desirable to those nearest to her person to die than to live without her!"*

---

* The Roman's exclamation and the answer of the loyal dying Charmian are taken literally from Plutarch's narrative.

The news of the death of their beloved, admired sovereign transformed Alexandria into a house of mourning. Obsequies of unprecedented magnificence and solemnity, at which many tears of sincere grief flowed, honoured her memory. One of Octavianus's most brilliant plans was frustrated by her death, and he had raved furiously when he read the letter in which Cleopatra, with her own hand, informed him of her intention to die. But he owed it to his reputation for generosity to grant her a funeral worthy of her rank. To the dead, who had ceased to be dangerous, he was ready to show an excess of magnanimity.

The treatment which he accorded to Cleopatra's children also won the world's admiration. His sister Octavia received them into her own house and intrusted their education to Archibius.

When the order to destroy the statues of Antony and Cleopatra was issued, Octavianus gave his contemporaries another proof of his disposition to be lenient, for he ordered that the numerous statues of the Queen in Alexandria and Egypt should be preserved. True, he had been influenced by the large sum of two thousand talents paid by an Alexandrian to secure this act of generosity. Archibius was the name of the rare friend who had impoverished himself to render this service to the memory of the beloved dead.

In later times the statues of the unfortunate

Queen adorned the places where they had been erected.

The sarcophagi of Cleopatra and Mark Antony, by whose side rested Iras and Charmian, were constantly heaped with flowers and offerings to the dead. The women of Alexandria, especially, went to the tomb of their beloved Queen as if it were a pilgrimage; but in after-days faithful mourners also came from a distance to visit it, among them the children of the famous lovers whom death here united—Cleopatra Selene, now the wife of the learned Numidian Prince Juba, Helios Antony, and Alexander, who had reached manhood. Their friend and teacher, Archibius, accompanied them. He taught them to hold their mother's memory dear, and had so reared them that, in their maturity, he could lead them with head erect to the sarcophagus of the friend who had confided them to his charge.

THE END.

D. APPLETON & CO.'S PUBLICATIONS.

THE SOVEREIGNS AND COURTS OF EUROPE. The Home and Court Life and Characteristics of the Reigning Families. By "POLITIKOS." With many Portraits. 12mo. Cloth, $1.50.

"A remarkably able book. . . . A great deal of the inner history of Europe is to be found in the work, and it is illustrated by admirable portraits."—*The Athenæum.*

"Its chief merit is that it gives a new view of several sovereigns. . . . The anonymous author seems to have sources of information that are not open to the foreign correspondents who generally try to convey the impression that they are on terms of intimacy with royalty."—*San Francisco Chronicle.*

"The anonymous author of these sketches of the reigning sovereigns of Europe appears to have gathered a good deal of curious information about their private lives, manners, and customs, and has certainly in several instances had access to unusual sources. The result is a volume which furnishes views of the kings and queens concerned far fuller and more intimate than can be found elsewhere."—*New York Tribune.*

". . . A book that would give the truth, the whole truth, and nothing but the truth (so far as such comprehensive accuracy is possible), about these exalted personages, so often heard about but so seldom seen by ordinary mortals, was a desideratum, and this book seems well fitted to satisfy the demand. The author is a well-known writer on questions indicated by his pseudonym."—*Montreal Gazette.*

"A very handy book of reference."—*Boston Transcript.*

MY CANADIAN JOURNAL, 1872–'78. By LADY DUFFERIN. Extracts from letters home written while Lord Dufferin was Governor-General of Canada. With Portrait, Map, and Illustrations from sketches by Lord Dufferin. 12mo. Cloth, $2.00.

"A graphic and intensely interesting portraiture of out-door life in the Dominion, and will become, we are confident, one of the standard works on the Dominion. . . . It is a charming volume."—*Boston Traveller.*

"In every place and under every condition of circumstances the Marchioness shows herself to be a true lady, without reference to her title. Her book is most entertaining, and the abounding good-humor of every page must stir a sympathetic spirit in its readers."—*Philadelphia Bulletin.*

"The many readers of Lady Dufferin's Journal of 'Our Vice-Regal Life in India' will welcome this similar record from the same vivacious pen, although it concerns a period antecedent to the other, and takes one back many years. The book consists of extracts from letters written home by Lady Dufferin to her friends (her mother chiefly) while her husband was Governor-General of Canada; and describes her experiences in the same chatty and charming style with which readers were before made familiar."—*Cincinnati Commercial-Gazette.*

New York: D. APPLETON & CO., 1, 3, & 5 Bond Street.

D. APPLETON & CO.'S PUBLICATIONS.

HANDY VOLUMES OF FICTION.

PEOPLE AT PISGAH. By Edwin W. Sanborn.
"A most amusing extravaganza."—*The Critic.*

MR. FORTNER'S MARITAL CLAIMS, and Other Stories. By Richard Malcolm Johnston.
"When the last story is finished we feel, in imitation of Oliver Twist, like asking for more."—*Public Opinion.*

GRAMERCY PARK. A Story of New York. By John Seymour Wood, author of "An Old Beau," etc.
"A realistic story of New York life, vividly drawn, full of brilliant sketches."—*Boston Advertiser.*

A TALE OF TWENTY-FIVE HOURS. By Brander Matthews and George H. Jessop.
"The reader finds himself in the midst of tragedy; but it is tragedy ending in comedy. The story is exceptionally well told."—*Boston Traveller.*

A LITTLE NORSK; or, Ol' Pap's Flaxen. By Hamlin Garland, author of "Main Traveled Roads," etc.
"There is nothing in story-telling literature to excel the naturalness, pathos, humor, and homelike interest with which the little heroine's development is traced."—*Brooklyn Eagle.*

TOURMALIN'S TIME CHEQUES. By F. Anstey, author of "Vice Versâ," "The Giant's Robe," etc.
"Each cheque is good for several laughs."—*New York Herald.*

FROM SHADOW TO SUNLIGHT. By the Marquis of Lorne.
"In these days of princely criticism—that is to say, criticism of princes—it is refreshing to meet a really good bit of aristocratic literary work, albeit the author is only a prince-in-law."—*Chicago Tribune.*

ADOPTING AN ABANDONED FARM. By Kate Sanborn.
"A sunny, pungent, humorous sketch."—*Chicago Times.*

ON THE LAKE OF LUCERNE, and Other Stories. By Beatrice Whitby.
"The stories are pleasantly told in light and delicate vein, and are sure to be acceptable to the friends Miss Whitby has already made on this side of the Atlantic."—*Philadelphia Bulletin.*

Each, 16mo, boards, with specially designed cover, 50 cents.

New York: D. APPLETON & CO., 1, 3, & 5 Bond Street.

D. APPLETON & CO.'S PUBLICATIONS.

HANDY VOLUMES OF FICTION.

Each, 12mo, flexible cloth, with special design, 75 cents.

THE TRANSLATION OF A SAVAGE. By GILBERT PARKER.

"To tell such a story convincingly a man must have what I call the rarest of literary gifts—the power to condense. Of the good feeling and healthy wisdom of this little tale others no doubt have spoken and will speak. But I have chosen this technical quality for praise, because in this I think Mr. Parker has made the furthest advance on his previous work. Indeed, in workmanship he seems to be improving faster than any of the younger novelists."—A. T. QUILLER-COUCH, *in the London Spectator.*

THE FAÏENCE VIOLIN. By CHAMPFLEURY. Translated by W. H. BISHOP.

"The style is happy throughout, the humorous parts being well calculated to bring smiles, while we can hardly restrain our tears when the poor enthusiast goes to excesses that have a touch of pathos."—*Albany Times-Union.*

TRUE RICHES. By FRANÇOIS COPPÉE.

"Delicate as an apple blossom, with its limp cover of pale green and its stalk of golden-rod, is this little volume containing two stories by François Coppée. The tales are charmingly told, and their setting is an artistic delight."—*Philadelphia Bulletin.*

"The author scarcely had a thought of sermonizing his readers, but each of these little stories presents a moral not easily overlooked, and whose influence lingers with those who read them."—*Baltimore American.*

A TRUTHFUL WOMAN IN SOUTHERN CALIFORNIA. By KATE SANBORN, author of "Adopting an Abandoned Farm," etc.

"The veracious writer considers the *pros* of the 'glorious climate' of California, and then she gives the *cons*. Decidedly the ayes have it. . . . The book is sprightly and amiably entertaining. The descriptions have the true Sanborn touch of vitality and humor."—*Philadelphia Ledger.*

A BORDER LEANDER. By HOWARD SEELY, author of "A Nymph of the West," etc.

"We confess to a great liking for the tale Mr. Seely tells. . . . There are pecks of trouble ere the devoted lovers secure the tying of their love-knot, and Mr. Seely describes them all with a Texan flavor that is refreshing."—*New York Times.*

"A swift, gay, dramatic little tale, which at once takes captive the reader's sympathy and holds it without difficulty to the end."—*Charleston News and Courier.*

New York: D. APPLETON & CO., 1, 3, & 5 Bond Street.

VALUABLE HAND-BOOKS.

Errors in the Use of English. By the late WILLIAM B. HODGSON, LL. D., Professor of Political Economy in the University of Edinburgh. American revised edition. 12mo, cloth, $1.50.

"This posthumous work of Dr. Hodgson deserves a hearty welcome, for it is sure to do good service for the object it has in view—improved accuracy in the use of the English language. . . . Perhaps its chief use will be in very distinctly proving with what wonderful carelessness or incompetency the English language is generally written. For the examples of error here brought together are not picked from obscure or inferior writings. Among the grammatical sinners whose trespasses are here recorded appear many of our best-known authors and publications."—*The Academy.*

The Orthoëpist: A Pronouncing Manual, containing about Four Thousand Five Hundred Words, including a Considerable Number of the Names of Foreign Authors, Artists, etc., that are often mispronounced. By ALFRED AYRES. Revised and Enlarged edition. 18mo, cloth, extra, $1.25.

"One of the neatest and most accurate pocket manuals on pronunciation. It ought to be on every library table."—*N. Y. Christian Advocate.*

The Verbalist: A Manual devoted to Brief Discussions of the Right and the Wrong Use of Words, and to some other Matters of Interest to those who would Speak and Write with Propriety, including a Treatise on Punctuation. By ALFRED AYRES, author of "The Orthoëpist." 18mo, cloth, extra, $1.00.

"A great deal that is worth knowing, and of which not even all educated people are aware, is to be learned from this well-digested little book."—*Philadelphia North American.*

The Rhymester; Or, THE RULES OF RHYME. A Guide to English Versification. With a Dictionary of Rhymes, an Examination of Classical Measures, and Comments upon Burlesque, Comic Verse, and Song-Writing. By the late TOM HOOD. Edited, with Additions, by Arthur Penn. Uniform with "The Verbalist." 18mo, cloth, gilt or red edges, $1.00.

"Ten or a dozen years ago, the late Tom Hood, also a poet, and the son of a poet, published 'The Rules of Rhyme,' of which we have a substantial reprint in 'The Rhymester,' with additions and side-lights from its American editor, Arthur Penn. The example of Hood's great father in his matchless melodies, his own skill as a cunning versifier, and the accomplished editing of Mr. Penn, have made this booklet a useful guide to English versification, the most useful one, indeed, that we are acquainted with."—*The Critic.*

For sale by all booksellers; or sent by mail, post-paid, on receipt of price.

New York: D. APPLETON & CO., 1, 3, & 5 Bond Street.

www.ingramcontent.com/pod-product-compliance
Lightning Source LLC
Chambersburg PA
CBHW031247250426
43672CB00029BA/1368